From Cr
Career

From Craft to Career

A Casting Director's Guide for the Actor

By
Merri Sugarman

With
Tracy Moss

methuen | drama

LONDON · NEW YORK · OXFORD · NEW DELHI · SYDNEY

METHUEN DRAMA
Bloomsbury Publishing Plc
50 Bedford Square, London, WC1B 3DP, UK
1385 Broadway, New York, NY 10018, USA
29 Earlsfort Terrace, Dublin 2, Ireland

BLOOMSBURY, METHUEN DRAMA and the Methuen Drama logo are
trademarks of Bloomsbury Publishing Plc

First published in Great Britain 2023

Cover design by Jess Stevens
Cover image: Compass icon stock illustration (© musmellow/iStock)

A catalogue record for this book is available from the British Library.

ISBN: HB: 978-1-3502-7602-4
PB: 978-1-3502-7601-7
ePDF: 978-1-3502-7604-8
eBook: 978-1-3502-7603-1

Typeset by Deanta Global Publishing Services, Chennai, India
Printed and bound in Great Britain

To find out more about our authors and books visit www.bloomsbury.com
and sign up for our newsletters.

"I'm always surprised by the stamina required to be behind the table; to be really present and available to each person who comes into the room. It's hard to feel the same about a scene after eight hours of listening to it over and over. I wish every audition could be at 11 am. But I draw strength from people like Merri Sugarman, who treats the last actor before dinner as enthusiastically as the first actor in the morning. If she can do it, day after day, year after year, then I can damn well do it too."

RICK ELICE, Tony Award Nominee for best book of a musical for Jersey Boys, Tony Award Nominee for best play and best original score written for the theater for Tony Award-winning play Peter and the Starcatcher, book writer of Tony Award-winning shows The Addams Family and The Cher Show

Contents

About the Authors ix
Foreword xi
Acknowledgments xiii

Introduction 1

1 My Path from Actor to Casting Director 4

Part 1 First Steps on the Career Path 9

2 How Do I Begin? 11

3 Where to Live? Why There? 15

4 Your Two Different Day Jobs 19

5 Where Do I Find the Work? 24

6 Curious Kids 35

Part 2 The Tools of the Trade 45

7 Pictures, Resumes, Reels, and Websites 47

8 Representation and Submissions 53

9 Unions: When It's Time to Join 60

10 Networking 65

11 Continuing Education 70

Part 3 The Casting Director's Role on the Creative Team 77

12 What, Exactly, Does a Casting Director Do? 79

13 The Casting Director and the Audition Process 86

Part 4 Auditions 97

14 Auditions: On Being Prepared 99

15 The Self-Tape Audition 117

16 In the Audition Room 122

Part 5 After the Audition 133

17 Booking It—Or Not 135

18 The First Day of School 145

19 Alternate Career Path? 151

20 That's a Wrap 155

Index 159

About the Authors

Merri Sugarman

Initially an actress (*Les Misérables, Aspects of Love*), Merri Sugarman found herself in Los Angeles, where she quickly made a name for herself at Liberman/Hirschfeld Casting working on such shows as *Seinfeld*, HBO's *Band of Brothers*, and the feature film *My Big Fat Greek Wedding*, to name a few. Following that, at Dreamworks Studios Merri was the Casting Executive in charge of TV Pilots and Series, including *Spin City* and the critically acclaimed *The Job*, starring Denis Leary. Time as Director of Casting for Dramas and Movies at ABC Television followed where she oversaw the casting of *Alias*, *NYPD Blue*, *The Practice*, and *The Music Man*, starring Matthew Broderick and Kristin Chenoweth, among many others.

After her years in LA, Merri moved back to New York City to coach one-on-one with actors, something she loves and still does as time permits. It was then that Tara Rubin offered her a Senior Casting Director position in which she cast the Broadway and touring companies of *Ain't Too Proud, Jersey Boys, Phantom of the Opera, Les Misérables, School of Rock, Miss Saigon*, and *A Bronx Tale*. Off Broadway work includes the musicals *Clueless* and *Trevor*. The Lyric Opera Chicago, The Goodman, and The Old Globe are among the many regional theaters Merri works with. She is the very proud casting director of the web series *Submissions Only*.

On a more personal note, Merri has been a Big Sister to Jenny since 2002 via the amazing Big Brothers/Big Sisters of America program, is a member of Who's Who in American Colleges and Universities, and was recognized with the Distinguished Alumni Award from Emerson College in 2021. Merri is a Tony Voter and a member of CSA (Casting Society of America).

Tracy Moss

Tracy Moss holds a degree in Dramatic Literature from New York University and has worked in a variety of capacities in television and film and on a very long list of Broadway shows and national tours, the first of which was the tour of *Les Misérables* where she and Merri met and became fast friends. She is delighted to have collaborated on this book and wholeheartedly recommends a life in the arts, whatever form that may take for each individual.

Foreword

By Tara Rubin

If you've ever seen a casting director portrayed in film or on TV, I can almost guarantee you that the character wasn't a nice person. In the movies, a casting director is invariably a gatekeeper: unapproachable, too busy and distracted to pay attention to an actor's work, and more focused on the actor's physical appearance than their talent. The movie scene will invariably involve an actor pouring their heart and soul into an audition while the casting director shuffles papers and reads their phone. At the end of the audition the casting director tells the actor she's "too blonde" or "not blonde enough." The actor leaves the audition feeling dejected and hopeless. The casting director moves on to the next actor—they have no real role in the creative process, they're just a gatekeeper whose only function is to control access to power.

If you're an actor, or hope to be one, I can assure you that casting directors like Merri Sugarman don't approach their work like the boorish casting directors in the movies. I've worked with Merri for almost twenty years—casting Broadway musicals, national tours, world premieres in regional theaters, and a film here and there. During that time, I've marveled at Merri's unwavering passion for the casting process and her dedication to the pursuit of the right actor for every role. She's relentlessly thorough in every casting search, not easily satisfied that she's found the right person, and remarkably open to seeing more and more actors until she feels she's identified the right set of candidates for a role. She holds herself and those she works with to a very high standard and creative teams—directors, choreographers, writers—consider her a true collaborator in the process of creating theater.

Merri understands that working with actors requires empathy and compassion. She's the actor's true advocate and doesn't hesitate to speak up for an actor who should remain in the running for a role, calls actors personally to give them helpful notes, and is conscientious about making sure actors have everything they need to be as successful as possible in the audition room. Merri, once an actor herself, just can't help but bring her humanity to her work. She also brings her strong sense of professionalism and arrives at each casting session with all of her materials in perfect order so the audition will run smoothly and each actor has the opportunity to be considered without distraction—no fumbling of papers or looking at phones. Her intense preparation and attention to detail create an atmosphere in which actors can shine.

Merri's book *From Craft to Career* was created to share her casting experience with actors, parents of actors, teachers of actors – anyone who is considering making the step to a professional career. Merri has compiled all the information you need to understand the business of this business, but *From Craft to Career* is more than a "how to audition" book. Merri explains the casting process from the perspective of the actor *and* the casting director in a way that will demystify what we do and help you identify the tools you need to navigate your career with confidence and success. She covers it all: audition preparation, callbacks, agents, unions, and self-tapes with her signature humor and pragmatism. *From Craft to Career* can be your guidebook now and in the years ahead. Good luck and I hope to see you in the audition room soon!

Acknowledgments

We would like to thank all the caring and brilliant professionals who allowed us to include their thoughtful and insightful responses to our questions about the industry, Tara Rubin—for her insight and humanity, Lorrie Lykins for her expert guidance and all of our friends and family whose patience and support has been invaluable. We would also like to thank the students—ALL of the students—who are the inspiration for this book.

Introduction

If you're reading this, you know you want to go pro. You're ready to launch your career as a professional actor but have no idea what steps to take.

Maybe you have an excellent education from a prestigious studio that provided training in the performing arts. Maybe you have a freshly minted degree in the performing arts from a college or conservatory. Maybe you've been doing community theater for years as a hobby and have a lot of talent and a lot of experience under your belt. Maybe you were a professional actor at one time but life took you in another direction and now you're ready to come back to the business.

Perhaps you're a parent who's paid a bundle for your child to earn a Bachelor of Fine Arts or Master's degree. Or, perhaps you have a child who has taken a passionate interest in performing on stage or on camera. You want to be supportive and help them achieve their goals but have no idea how to do that in any practical way. You don't know what it takes to help them get a job.

That's why I wrote this book. The information I'm sharing with you will help you to understand the landscape of this amazing industry and how to navigate getting work in it. No matter your path to this point, the question remains the same: How do I get a job as a professional actor?

You probably already know that the very first step to getting a job as a professional actor is the audition. My goal is to demystify the casting process—to help you understand what's happening on the other side of the audition table so that you can be ready from the moment you walk in to your audition to the moment you get the call saying you booked the job and for every step in between. I'll break down the diverse casting needs of film, television, and legit (live professional) theater in a way that will be easy to understand. Promise.

All the talent in the world won't help you get a job if you aren't effective at the *business* part of the business. Without the tools to pursue the work, all of your talent, ambition and passion won't help you make a living. How much effort you put into carrying out all this work is up to you. Just remember, when you notice someone whom you may think is less talented than you booking more jobs than you, it's possible it is because they work harder at the business of the business and it's paying off.

And I know first-hand that it's hard work. I, too, started out in the entertainment industry as an actress—which is not unusual in and of itself for a casting director—except that I transitioned to a career in casting quite late, not to mention that I did have some success as a working actor.

It's because of my experience as a former actor who spent years pounding the pavement and after that, years on the other side of the table as a casting director working on virtually every level of casting there is in the entertainment industry, that I understand the need for a broader education on the business of the business.

I've been lucky enough to be invited to teach many types of classes and workshops at a wide variety of wonderful schools. Educators and administrators from colleges, conservatories, and all manner of professional training programs have me in to teach because they recognize that the knowledge I bring to the table—how to go about getting a job—is tantamount to an actor's fundamental education.

Teachers are the bedrock of your success in honing your craft and your art but as a casting director and as a *business*woman,

I'm always delighted when an educator brings me in to teach their students how to bridge the gap between craft and career. In fact, it was my experiences during those classes that initially inspired me to assemble the "business of the business" information into book form. Whether or not you have a formal education in the arts or are simply gifted and have a passion for performing, the information in this book will help you navigate your way to a professional career.

There are boatloads of things actors will never have any control over but there are also a lot of things they *can* control—they just don't know it. I *want* you to know what those things are.

As you take the going-pro journey, you'll find that everyone you encounter will have different ideas about how best to go about getting work and no one is all right or all wrong. You'll start seeing what works for you very quickly and that's all that matters in the end. I'm here to give you a jumping-off point and tools to help guide you toward your goal—going pro as an actor.

1 My Path from Actor to Casting Director

I want to take some time to tell you a little about my journey from being a professional actor to being a casting director so that you'll have enough insight into my background that you'll trust I know what I'm talking about—that I've walked in your shoes in some way—and that it'll be worth your time to read on. If you take away any small measure of encouragement from learning about how I found my way to this point in *my* career that serves you in some way on *your* journey, then the telling is worthwhile.

I was an actress when I was a little girl. Not professionally. Just in my mind. I had a huge flair for the dramatic, a need for attention and a big voice, so I naturally fell in with other kids of like mind. Be it at the piano at home, the synagogue or family weddings, I'd sing anywhere anyone would let me. If I could get someone to sit and watch and listen—that was pretty much all I needed.

While it never even occurred to me to "go pro" as a child, I was lucky to have parents who were supportive and encouraged my love for the arts. I attended performing arts summer camps, participated in All-State and All-American choirs, drama clubs, and finally earned a Bachelor of Fine Arts in Musical Theater from Emerson College, Boston.

After graduation, I moved to New York City. I had no doubt that it was the place for me. I got a job as a waitress, moved into a tiny one-bedroom fifth-floor walk-up in the West Village with a roommate, and set out to pursue my dreams.

I worked very hard, paid a lot of dues, and auditioned for everything and anything I could. I auditioned several times for, and was finally cast in, the third national tour of *Les Misérables* and after that, Andrew Lloyd Webber's musical *Aspects of Love*. I was very grateful that I had long runs in two era-defining shows but every time a contract ended, I went back to waitressing and doing other odd jobs. I continued to take voice lessons and acting classes but after many years of a decent amount of success as a professional actor, I was less than enthusiastic about my career. I struggled with an increasing sense of apathy for something I'd loved for so long.

Because I hadn't booked another job as quickly as I felt I deserved at that point in my career (and yes, it's true, every actor thinks that every job they book will be their last), I fell into a pretty deep depression and realized I needed a change. A big one. I thought a change in scenery would do the trick. As an actor, unless you've already been or you're from there, you're always wondering whether you should try Los Angeles—or New York if you've already tried Los Angeles. I moved to Los Angeles mostly because an agent who had seen me in the *Aspects of Love* tour had offered to represent me in Los Angeles if I ever made my way to the West Coast. Also, a friend there had an extra bedroom. So, I shipped some stuff, sold some stuff and got on a plane. When I got there, I bought a clunker of a car that lasted about a year before it bit the dust and used the last of my tour savings to buy a new one, got a hostess job at a trendy restaurant in the Valley and took up residence in "Beverly Hills Adjacent." And I do mean *adjacent*. I studied for my California driver's license, found a day job, and went to work looking for an acting job. It wasn't bad. But it wasn't good. Once again, I really started to question my choices career-wise. I was well into my thirties by then and to be fair—I'd started questioning my passion for the actor's life even while I'd been working as one. *Not* being passionate about your career is the biggest dead end ever and really a waste of valuable time. The thrill was gone even when I was working. Those were all pretty obvious distress signals.

I began asking myself what made me happy. This was hard because if I really answered honestly, it might mean I had to change the course of my whole life—which might mean I'd be embarrassed, I'd have to admit I'd failed in some way (which ultimately is only about our own perception of what success means, but I didn't know that until much later).

Around that time a friend who was producing a sitcom mentioned that the casting company working on his show was looking for an assistant. He knew I'd been feeling pretty lost and wondered if casting was something I might want to look into. I interviewed and I promptly became the oldest living assistant on the planet.

I fetched food and cut sides (sides are excerpts of scripts for audition purposes) for bosses who were, in many instances, ten years younger than me. Humbling. But I discovered that I'm a girl who likes a steady paycheck. Plus, I was getting it—this "casting" thing. I think my maturity ultimately helped me move up fairly quickly. I knew to keep my mouth shut and my eyes and my ears open. I soaked it all in. I was promoted. I learned how it worked in TV and film—not only about the audition process in that arena but also about the contracts and the politics and the business aspects of it all.

And so there ensued a series of timely events that brought me to the executive casting departments at Dreamworks Studios and then to ABC Television. Who knew there were so many ways to be a casting director?

Suffice it to say, an office overlooking the Hollywood sign and a car that didn't embarrass me at the valet—plus getting to work with some really creative and groundbreaking people—did *not* suck.

I went into the arts because I loved the creative endeavor but once you're an executive the stakes are very high and you are answerable to a host of people in a very corporate environment. I adapted and did very well but by the end of two years at the network, I knew this was not the environment for me. It became clear to me that the farther I got from being allowed to simply hunt for talent, the farther I got from a sense of purpose and contentment. In fact, it was during my time as a network casting director that it became clear that all I really wanted was to help actors get jobs and contribute to the creative process while doing so.

While I certainly came into my own professionally in Los Angeles and had a very happy existence there for eight years—the longest I'd ever stayed anywhere in my adult life—I never felt like my skin fit quite right there. I think I started, albeit subconsciously, yearning for New York pretty early on in my time there.

Ultimately, I left Los Angeles behind and moved back to New York and went to work at a friend's wedding photography studio. I started up my audition workshops for actors and I coached them in my living room on the side. I loved doing it and my clients seemed gratified and kept coming back but it wasn't enough to earn a living and I quickly realized that unless I was in a position to help people get jobs—that is, if I was still *casting*—no one was all that interested in what I had to say. Fair enough. It's a business. I got it. But I didn't miss the casting business as I knew it and so I happily ensconced myself with bridal event planners and left the rest behind. Except not really.

My heart was still with the theater, so I got involved with a nonprofit organization that gave kids interested in the arts the opportunity to learn by working with theater professionals via after-school programs at places that they couldn't otherwise afford. I met a kid who was interested in casting and I called Tara Rubin—the person who'd cast me in practically everything I'd ever done as an actor—and asked if she needed an intern. She didn't. What she did need was a casting director and she made me an offer. Now if it had been anyone else, I'm not sure I'd have entertained the idea of going back into casting. But this was casting for *Broadway*. This was where my heart lived! These were my people! Could this really be happening? More significantly, it was Tara Rubin. I knew that working with Tara was something I could wrap my head, and heart, around.

I accepted the offer from Tara and never looked back. Getting to that point was a much more emotional journey than I've laid out here—there were classes and teachers and auditions and agents and mentors and pictures and resumes and introspection and sickness and good fortune and the *work* of it all—but there you have it—*the road that led me here*. And by "here" I mean casting a new Broadway musical, writing a book, requesting my Tony Voter tickets, getting ready for a slew of teaching gigs, and just feeling so grateful for all of it.

Okay, let's get going.

Part 1
First Steps on the Career Path

2 How Do I Begin?

This road you've chosen is not an easy one to navigate. There are many obstacles to overcome and big life decisions to make along the way. But, how to begin?

First and foremost, ask yourself what kind of a career you want to have. Are you looking for fame? Magazine covers? Is your financial security, your partner's (and maybe your kids'), being figured into your decisions? Do you want to coach your child's soccer leagues equally as much as you want to make a living doing what you love? Always keep in mind that there are *many* ways to have a career in show business, that there is not just one road to success and that success professionally means nothing without success personally.

Ironically, it was when I decided to quit show business that my professional acting career began. I had finally earned my Equity card but hadn't booked a job for *a long freakin' time*. Like *a year*. I started asking myself what the hell I was doing—not just what I was doing *wrong* but what I was *doing*.

During that period of struggling, I had an opportunity to be a drama counselor at a summer camp in Colorado. So off I went to Grand Junction where I led theater games with kids who just wanted to have fun. I spent my spare time wandering the woods listening to sad songs through my headphones and wondering what the hell to do with my life. I was twenty-five and summer camp was definitely over. I decided to quit pursuing acting as a career but had no other plan.

When I got back home to New York, I picked up a slightly out-of-date copy of Backstage, the printed trade publication for auditions back then—habit—and saw that there'd been auditions for the third national touring company of *Les Misérables* while I'd been away. Now I'd been to countless auditions for that show. And nothin'. Still, I was disappointed that I'd missed the latest round of auditions so I decided to make one more push and to do something out of the ordinary—and also kind of taboo—but I had nothing to lose. I called the casting director's office. This was pre-email, so calling was quasi-acceptable at the time, but I emphatically do *not* recommend that route now.

Johnson-Liff Casting was the premier casting company for theater at the time. It was the 1980s and we were seeing *Cats*, *Les Misérables*, *Miss Saigon*, *Phantom of the Opera*, *Starlight Express*, and *Sunset Boulevard* all for the first time and they were casting them *all*.

I was hoping to get Tara Rubin (who was then a casting assistant at Johnson-Liff) on the phone to see if I could get an appointment for the *Les Misérables* callbacks. But Andy Zerman himself picked up the phone. I came to adore Andy but, in that moment, he was all business. Andy asked, "Merri where do you see yourself in this show?" Subtext in my mind: "Merri, you've auditioned *five* times. If it hasn't happened yet, why do you think it will happen now?" I honestly don't remember my exact answer but I remember thinking, "I can sing this show. It moves me. I want to tell that story. You haven't seen what I'm capable of." I must have answered in that vein and Andy said he'd keep me in mind and hung up.

That extra push, that risk, paid off. The next day I got a call from Tara Rubin with an appointment to come in for one more audition. I truly believe that the reason I got that appointment, other than my cheeky phone call of the day before, was because Tara and her colleagues had seen me at auditions for other shows. And they saw something in me and they *remembered* me. Also, that day's session was seeing a lot of cancellations and the casting assistants were filling the time slots as fast as they could.

Okay, so the good news, great actually, was that I got myself an audition for *Les Mis*. The bad news was that it was *that* very day. In two hours. On stage at Broadway's Golden Theater. I took a shower, grabbed my book of audition songs, and spent all my remaining cash for the week on a taxi to the theater.

I'd decided last minute to change it up from what I'd shown them before. They say the definition of insanity is doing the same thing over and over again and expecting different results. So, this time I'd show 'em how funny I was instead of pulling out the same heart-wrenching (apparently *not*) ballads I'd done for them in the past.

As I said, I had just returned from summer camp. I also need to mention that I had a cast on my leg from a horseback riding accident. Still, with my head held high, I clomped up onto the stage of a Broadway theater for the first time in my life, got a chair, and used it to hoist myself up into a sitting position on top of the piano. I posed, nodded to the accompanist—who looked absolutely horrified—and began to sing a comedic song that I hoped and prayed would get some laughs. It did.

At the end of the song, I clumsily slid off the piano. They asked me what else I had. I sang a ballad. A ballad that obviously had been heard a million times before by this group of casting directors. A ballad so long that before I even started, I could see Andy Zerman waving his hands in the universal casting director code for, "Sweet Jesus, *anything* but that!"

When I finished, John Caird, associate director of the Royal Shakespeare Company, Tony and Olivier Award-winning director for *Nicholas Nickleby*, Outer Critics Circle Award for Outstanding Director of a musical and Best Director Tony Award winner for *Les Misérables* (and who had scores of shows and awards yet to come), jumped up on stage, asked me to pull up a chair, knelt at my feet and proceeded to ask me some questions.

I remembered nothing of the last ten minutes, but once I was able to collect myself, it seemed to me that he was asking questions unrelated to the audition and I was confused. "Do you have a boyfriend?""Children?""How do you feel about children?" For the life of me I could not figure out his reason for asking these questions and I *so* wanted to give him the right answers! Come to find out he was trying to assess just how ready, willing, and able I was to leave my friends and family and New York for a long period of time.

John and I finished our chat. Everyone said thanks. I said thanks. I left—limping and dragging my right ankle behind thinking, "Well, that was different . . . but I've been here before." The next day I got the call offering me the tour of *Les Mis*. I had finally booked it. That was a good day.

Okay. I wasn't quitting so fast. I toured. I put away money. I saw the country. I made life-long friends. I learned a lot. Most importantly, I learned to keep my options open and to keep moving forward.

That story is the long way to say the key to taking the first (or next) step in your career is to constantly begin again. Take each day and each decision as it comes. If you truly and continuously check in with yourself, ask yourself questions about your mental, physical and spiritual health, and then assess the situation— where you are in your life *and* career, the answers will come.

Always remember that just when you think you've exhausted every resource at your disposal to get a job, if you keep moving forward, mind open, following your instincts and your heart, the next opportunity will come along in due course.

3 Where to Live? Why There?

So now you're ready to pursue a professional career. You've saved up enough money to move to the city—any city where you might find work—and it's time to decide where to live and why *that* city.

I happen to think a lot of actors go to New York or Los Angeles before they should. It's hard to have specific long-term goals, but what you must have is a pretty good handle on who you are and what creature comforts you need to thrive. There is great work being done all over this country: New York, Philadelphia, Chicago, Minneapolis, Seattle, Oregon, and Los Angeles—all good choices. If you're more comfortable starting out in a smaller market and working your way to Chicago, Los Angeles, or New York, that's great.

Making the leap from *any* arena to the next is frightening and uncomfortable. Now that you're going pro, you're going to be a much smaller fish in a much bigger pond. And because of this, certain ideas will begin to take shape that you'll need to address. How will you earn money? Where will you live? Where do you see yourself? What kind of a career do you want to have?

Try and do some creative visualization. You want to set yourself up to succeed and settling someplace because it's where you think you're *supposed* to go is not a good reason to go.

There'll be nerves and challenges all along the way in every new city. When everything's new it is incredibly hard and exhausting.

Try not to give yourself more than you know you can handle and *really* try not to compare yourself to anyone else.

New York?

New York is either very cold or very hot (except for two days of spring and two days of fall). The subways are filthy, scary and confusing. You have to carry around a huge bag all day every day and spend $20 on a sandwich, chips and a drink for lunch sometimes. That said, the old adage is true, "If you can make it there, you'll make it anywhere." I speak from experience having lived and worked on both coasts for long periods of time.

Only in New York will you really get the opportunity to audition, even without representation, almost every day if you're of a mind to do so. There are open calls and Actor's Equity union calls (where non-union actors can and will often be seen when time permits). There are extras companies you can register with. Working as an extra as your temp job can help pay the bills and you get to be on a set and watch and learn.

In New York, nearly everyone serious about their careers is in class at least some of the time and you'll meet people and hear about opportunities there that you wouldn't otherwise—like someone you went to college with just became an agent. An actor is taking a leave from a show and there are auditions for her replacement happening. The guy next to you knows about some lucrative part time seasonal work.

There is more film and television being shot in New York than ever before. Pilot season happens in New York just as it does in Los Angeles and is year-round nowadays.

If you can figure out your finances in order to be in the thick of it in New York, for full immersion, there's no other place like it.

Los Angeles?

Los Angeles is obviously the mecca for film and television. It is a car culture and altogether a gentler lifestyle with weather that makes you feel like you're in paradise. So, for some, it's a far better place to start because it's all a little slower and more relaxed. Maybe you're more comfortable with that pace and vibe.

If you've got an agent who's really paying you some attention, you might get audition appointments on a regular basis. But because usually you won't get through any doors there without an agent or knowing someone—a casting director, or the producer (who is maybe the father of the kid you're babysitting)—someone involved somehow with the project to help you get a foot in the door—your opportunities to audition will be fewer and farther between.

I am in no way knocking Los Angeles—it's beautiful and there is a lot of amazing and undeniably creative work being done there. It's just going to be even more challenging there to create your own work and get people to see it.

Los Angeles is known for some wonderful improv schools. Whether or not you consider yourself funny, take an improv class. Improv is a great leveler—you have to perform, you have to write, you have to follow rules, you have to work well with others, you have to be in the moment, and you have to listen. Improv is a great way to keep your skills sharp and to continue to grow as a performer. In fact, take an improv class no matter where you end up living.

All the Places in Between?

Chicago is known for its deep-dish pizza. It's also rich with regional and repertory theaters. For some people it's a better comfort zone than New York or Los Angeles and the opportunities to audition and perform are many and varied.

I have pals who are married and raising children and living a basically suburban existence as artists in residence at the Stratford Festival in Canada, the Guthrie in Minneapolis, the 5th Avenue Theater in Seattle, and at the Oregon Shakespeare Festival. Similar lifestyle opportunities can be found in Las Vegas with Cirque du Soleil and with the company of a Broadway sit-down (a Broadway show that is playing for more than a couple of weeks in any given city, but usually larger cities like Chicago, San Francisco, Los Angeles, and Las Vegas).

You *can* have a lovely life of art *and* backyard barbecues. While you may well eventually achieve this lifestyle wherever you are, it happens more easily and far more quickly in cities and towns other than New York and Los Angeles.

I cannot stress enough that wherever it is that you decide to begin the journey, you know what triggers your biggest fears and anxieties and you should set yourself up for success by going wherever it is that you don't think you'll be utterly paralyzed by the daily ins and outs of living.

While you don't have to decide right now *exactly* what kind of a career you want—you should have *some* self-knowledge, right? Just make the best choice for you in the moment.

If you try one place and it doesn't pan out—you haven't failed. Take the lessons learned and move on. Try someplace else. Follow your own path.

4 Your Two Different Day Jobs

Your Survival Day Job

While working toward the first acting job or even while between acting jobs, you will need to find a way to pay the bills. It's time to get a survival job.

After the *Aspects of Love* tour came to a close, I asked myself if I'd become one of those actors who didn't actually need a day job anymore and reached the conclusion that since the percentage of those people seemed to be in the negative numbers, I knew I still had to figure out a way to keep money coming in. I had some savings but I wasn't about to plow through them. Waitressing was what I knew how to do. I filled out applications at every place from the deli on my corner to The Rainbow Room. I got something in between and tried not to get too depressed as I married ketchups and wiped down syrup holders. And I started auditioning. Again.

I had to pay the rent and presumably, so do you. Even if money is not an issue for you, honestly, it should be—how to make it, how to save it, how to handle it.

If you're just out of school and have your mom's credit card—great. You're lucky. Use it to help you with voice lessons and scene study classes and, by all means, treat yourself to a massage or a gym membership. But *get a job* and pay your own bills. You're an adult. Working is good. It builds character. It raises the stakes.

What kinds of jobs might give you the freedom to pursue acting work?

Waiting tables is back-breaking work but the money's good and the hours are flexible and there's a good chance your co-workers will want your shifts when you have an audition and they'll need you to take theirs when they get one. A restaurant job will mean you're memorizing lines and learning music at 2:00 a.m. Well, okay, that's part of what you signed up for when you decided to go pro.

There are many online work-from-home jobs like proofreading and music transcription that you can do on your own schedule. If you read music, you'd be a great help to composers, music directors and music librarians. Apply for a hotel concierge gig. Love to clean out your closets? Go organize someone else's. Babysitters make decent money. Clean apartments. Be a telemarketer. Get a taxi driver's license. Own a car?—Uber and Lyft. Can you sew? Hang pictures? Do any and all of that for profit. Go sing in a wedding band or better yet, find a job that gets you an insider's view of the industry. Bartend at a theater, sell merchandise or usher. Be a personal assistant to any industry professional.

Jobs are *everywhere*! Do some research, find a good fit and get to work.

Your Actual Day Job—Being a Professional Actor

An actor is never truly out of work if the actor is always looking for work. Looking for work *is a job* and should be treated as such. What brings actors down so quickly is *not* having auditions, *not* getting callbacks when you do have auditions, *not* booking the jobs from those callbacks. And often that cycle can last a long time. You must fill those hours. Just because you are in a moment when you are not being paid to act, it doesn't mean you rest.

There are so many ways to create your own work. Be inventive! Get together with pals and read a play out loud and invite a handful of people who might be connected to a handful of other people or even connected themselves somehow—in any way—to industry people. Or rent a studio and do a scene night and make everyone involved sign a contract that ensures they are responsible for bringing at least two industry folks in to see it.

One of the things I did to fill my time was to put together a showcase for myself. Cabaret was and still is a great way to create your own work and get seen by industry people. I had a ball doing it. I mean, I just sang songs that I loved. I used a lot of props—berets, long cigarette holders, boas—you get the picture. But for one night I was the star. While that part of it may seem self-indulgent, I learned so much about what it takes to produce a show. I had to pay an accompanist and I had to guarantee a certain amount of money at the door *and* pay for my own club soda. It was worth every penny. Absolutely *nothing* came of this except a full house of adoring fans, aka my family and friends, and a much-needed confidence boost. Sometimes you just do stuff because you're challenged by it and you grow from it and that is enough.

Since you may not have a place to go to every day where you'll be working toward getting your next (or your first) professional acting job—you *must* develop the discipline to make the pursuit of happiness (*working as a professional actor*) part of your daily routine.

Half the working actors out there are less talented than you. The harsh reality is that they often have more success than you because they work harder at *getting work* than you do. *This* you *can* control. Here's how:

1. Do a mailing a day. Picture/Resume in an envelope addressed to an actual person with the name of the project you are self-submitting for. Forget the cover

letter—a post-it™ with a quick salutation and *maybe* a note will suffice. If you have mutual friends or you want to invite them to something you have coming up, then a brief note is fine. As you begin to meet casting directors and agents and producers and directors—*stay in touch with them*. It may feel like you're spinning your wheels but if just *one* of these relationships leads to an audition or a job then it's worth it.

2. If you've met *anyone* even remotely in the business you should have gotten that person's contact information. Depending on the circumstances, you should follow that up with either a thank you note or a postcard with your headshot on it as a reminder of who you are, where, when, and how you met and a reiteration that you're going to keep in touch. It could be that the host of the dinner party you attended last night as someone's plus one is a producer. Maybe the guy you met at a political rally mentioned his friend is on the creative team of *Hamilton* and will introduce the two of you. Perhaps your headshot photographer hired you to hold his equipment when he shot the wedding of a Tony Award-winning director's daughter. Later you got to meet the father of the bride and now he'll remember you when you follow up. Maybe while working that restaurant job, you waited on the table of a producer and helped him show his guests a wonderful time—he'll remember you—send a note with a picture and resume. Your actor friend heard his agent lost a client who is your type and tells you about it—you now know there may be a place for you at that agency. Then you send along your picture and resume with a brief note, get an interview and wind up signing with that agency. It's all *Six Degrees of Separation!*

Be relentless yet strategic with the stuff that is tangible and clear. The lists, the correspondence—*it's the follow-up that never ends.* Seriously, keep in touch with anyone who has been or is likely *to help in any way at all, all while keeping a professional distance.*

3. If you're in musical theater you must *sing. Every. Damn. Day.* Seriously. *Sing every day.* Always be working on something new. *Always.* Once you've added a song to your book and you've perfected it—get to work on a new one. Your work is never done.

4. Stretch, run, work out, go to dance class, do yoga, do Pilates, do something—*anything*—that keeps you fit and healthy. *Every Day.*

5. Learn to play an instrument. The more you bring to the table, the more chances you'll have to get a job. Learn to play the guitar, ukulele, piano, trumpet, drums—anything. Root through your basement at home and find the recorder you played in your fifth grade Spring Chorus Concert. Try and be capable on *some* instrument. Personality emerges when we watch someone playing an instrument. Trust me. It'll come in handy. Or maybe it will just make you feel good. Either way, it's a win-win.

There. Five things for you to do every day to keep your business plan on track and moving forward.

Keep a checklist and make these things as big a priority as if it were your money job—because frankly unless you're signing a contract—that *is* your job. And once you book a job, keep it up. All jobs end. It's the career that endures and it's your job to carry on with it.

At the end of the day, doing those tasks may not always feel like progress and may even seem like busywork but it can't hurt and will most probably give you a leg up even if you don't know how or when. Also, there is dignity in discipline.

5 Where Do I Find the Work?

The path from honing a craft to having a career in any art form is different for everyone. Many actors have thriving acting careers within their hometown community and are happy to shine in their local market on both amateur and professional levels. Others choose to take the skills they've learned on a local level to move on to other training grounds in larger markets as a means to their end goal of performing on Broadway or in a television series or a major motion picture. No matter your goal, the first step toward landing work as an actor is always the audition.

Once you start looking you might be surprised to find that opportunities to audition, to act, and to gain experience, are everywhere. And you will find an infinite number of resources available to you. First of all, focus on exposure to industry people. Expose yourself to, and participate in, the world around you. If you tell one person, just one—maybe at church or on your way out of a yoga class—that you want to look into some local acting opportunities they very well may have a suggestion for you on how to get involved or they might know someone who can help you do so. Being curious and asking questions are your very first steps into the world known as networking. Keep being curious and keep asking questions—it will serve you well.

You can have success looking for acting work in any city. You don't have to be in the epicenters of the industry—Los Angeles or Chicago or New York or any other big cosmopolitan city for that matter. You can find auditions and work if you're a child who has developed an interest in acting, if you've taken a break from the business to raise a family, or if you've just graduated from college and moved home to sock away some money.

You can find auditions if you've just retired from a completely different career and want to dabble in the arts, and even if you're a seasoned professional who wants or needs to step away from the big leagues and you just want to continue to enjoy the craft.

Here are some places to start looking and some information on how the audition and casting processes may differ between them.

Local High Schools and Local Colleges and Universities

Get an email address from their websites for someone in the theater, broadcast or film departments and write to them. Ask them if they need any "locals" in any of their upcoming projects. If you get a positive answer, be sure to carefully follow their instructions on how to go about auditioning.

Community Theater

Do an online search for "Local Theater Auditions" or "Open Calls for local shows." It may help to type in your city or your zip code. (If you just search for "local theaters" you'll probably get movie theaters and concert halls, which isn't really what you're looking for.) The theaters that come up will have websites with their season of shows listed. Even if there are no audition postings, heck, even if there's no actual website, get a phone number and call their main office. Tell them you are an actor based in the area (or that your kid is) and you'd like to know how their auditions work. Ask who you might be able to get in touch with to volunteer for the theater as a way to introduce yourself and become immersed in the community. Call your church or your community or recreational center or a local dance school and ask if they have any productions coming up. Ask what the casting process is and follow up accordingly.

Dinner Theater

Dinner Theater is a format that combines a meal with a live stage play or musical. Often Dinner Theaters are "Equity houses" (meaning they must hire a certain amount of union actors), but usually there are plenty of openings for local, non-union actors. You'll follow the same steps to get information as you did for community theaters.

- Auditions for Community Theater and Dinner Theater
  You don't need to worry too much about having a professional picture and resume to give them. You can take some shots with your phone and have them printed out as an 8 × 10 photo. They're just for reference. Same with the resumes. We all know you've got to start somewhere and you may only have a few or no acting credits. Staple your photo back-to-back with a piece of 8 × 10 paper that includes your name and phone number and email address. If you do have any prior experience as an actor, you should show that as well. List the title of the show, the role you played, and where you performed the show.
  As far as the auditions themselves—they will probably be pretty cut and dried. Community theater auditions are usually conducted during an open call when anyone can show up and audition. If it's for a dinner theater, they may make an appointment time for your audition and may even send you some scenes from the play to learn. For both, if it's a musical, they may ask you to bring sheet music for an accompanist to play while you sing a song or they may, especially for children, simply ask you to sing something like *Happy Birthday* to get an idea of

your vocal sound and ability. Or, they may ask for both. If it's a musical there may also be a dance audition where they will teach you some dance steps or more complex choreography. After the initial audition, there may be a callback where they ask you to learn some more material (dialogue or music) or they just bring you back in to do the same thing you did the first time. There's no time limit on how long it might take them to make their decisions but you can be pretty sure that if you don't hear anything within a month or so you haven't been cast. You probably won't get any feedback or reasons why you didn't get the job. That's show biz.

Local Television

There are a variety of ways to go here. Every city has a local cable access show—maybe it's a children's program, maybe it's a news hour. If television is of interest to you, find out if any of your local stations use volunteers or interns. If you've never been in a television studio, try to take a tour to get the lay of the land. You could be a volunteer they use to run errands, hold cue cards (big signs with the words the hosts or actors are to speak written on them), print scripts, enter data—who knows? Again, the best way to get information on how to go about finding out more is to do an internet search and follow the clues. Networking can be really useful locally too. Perhaps someone in your circle of friends works in television or radio locally or knows someone who does. You'll likely be surprised by how much information on auditions for local television you'll get by networking.

Often in smaller cities and towns the local car dealership or pet shelter or storage place or any number of other businesses will use local actors for their on-air talent for commercials. Frequently they use their friends and family in the commercials and sometimes they call a local talent agency and ask them to send over their clients' pictures and resumes or some examples of their clients' work on video. To really get going in this kind of television work, you may find you need an agent in order to get in the mix for these things. Online searches for commercial auditions might lead you to something, but opportunities of this kind will usually come via representation (agents) for professional actors.

Cabaret

Create your own work. You can do this anywhere and you'll find it an invaluable learning experience both for performing and what it takes to produce the work. You can build your show around whatever you're passionate about or the skill set unique to you. For inspiration go to comedy clubs or cabarets in your town. Go to the open mic night at your local karaoke bar. Check out what people are doing in those venues and where you might fit in.

Improv

I recommend anyone interested in any type of performing go find themselves a beginning improvisation class. You're given case scenarios and you've got about ten seconds to create a story with your scene partner(s). The process is scary because you have to think on your feet, break out of your shell, work well with others, and really listen. Almost every town I've ever been to boasts an improv class. Maybe it's part of an afternoon program for tweens or teens. Maybe the community center has adult continuing education classes and next semester someone's coming in to teach in improv class. You won't know until you go looking.

Some famous improv organizations include The Groundlings, Second City and Upright Citizens Brigade. You'll find most of these in major cities like Chicago, New York, Los Angeles, Minneapolis, Atlanta, and Austin. If you visit those cities, take in a performance or research them online and study clips where you can.

Professional Regional Theaters

Truly you can find out about these auditions in exactly the same way you looked for Community and Dinner Theater information. And again—the audition process will approximate the ones already discussed. The difference here is that these theaters will usually be presenting shows that are designed and performed by professionals. In these productions however, there are usually a limited number of roles that are reserved for locally based actors. It's smart business for these theaters to hire local actors since they are a lot less costly—no travel, no housing, no per diem (daily stipend for meals, travel and housing costs—per day) involved.

Broadway League Local Venues

Many cities are home to facilities that present national tours of Broadway shows and many other large-scale touring productions, shows on ice, the circus, and so on. These venues can be great resources for local performers so keep an eye on the shows scheduled to appear in your town. During the holiday season, many of these professional companies utilize local choirs and will hire children and adults to fill out the company in smaller roles that can be easily rehearsed in a short time frame. For instance, ballet companies performing *The Nutcracker* will bring in people from local dance studios to perform all the roles aside from those of the principal dancers. And some Broadway touring shows, like (at the time of this writing) *Waitress* and *Finding Neverland,* will hire locals to perform the child roles in each city. Try to learn about the shows coming to your town and educate yourself about any opportunities that they might bring with them.

Summer Theater (Summer Stock)

There are hundreds of these theaters in the United States. Professional actors come from all over to live and work on the premises of these venues for three months or so—usually in June, July, and August. The theaters tend to band together to audition and interview candidates for positions in summer (and year-round) professional theaters as performers. They have apprentice programs and often hire interns. Sometimes the kid running the box office will be needed for a one-line part, so he'll do one job by day and another by night. It's a rich training ground for performers of all ages and experience levels.

Check out the following websites (you can even register online to audition):

- NETCs (New England Theater Conference): https://www.netconline.org/netc-theater-auditions
- SETCs (Southeastern Theater Conference): https://www.setc.org/auditions/
- STRAWHATS: https://strawhat-auditions.com/public/

Theater Festivals

There is a theater festival going on somewhere all the time. They may not be happening in your area right this minute, or in your area at all, but keep them on your radar. Do some digging and find out what they're all about. It may be that a director from your area is having some success and being featured in big festivals and while there may not be opportunities to insert yourself into *those* festivals as actors, *that* director will be coming back home to direct shows. That presents learning opportunities on the local level.

There are festivals for virtually every type of theater; from puppetry to playwriting, they present a wide variety of performance opportunities for actors.

Start your research with these few types of festivals and major events:

- RENAISSANCE FESTIVALS and the like, while not necessarily presenting plays, often hire local people to dress up in the costumes of the era and wander around as part of creating the "atmosphere" they are trying to achieve. Maybe it's not "acting" as you've been thinking of it but there's an "audience" of fair-goers and your job is to help them feel like they're really in the 1500s for a day. Fun!

- SHAKESPEARE FESTIVALS—sometimes these "seasons" are six to eight months long. Usually there is a Repertory Company—a troupe of actors who play different roles in all the plays. Sometimes they'll use locals as part of the crowd scenes or even in small roles.

- New York Musical Festival (NYMF): http://www.nymf.org/

- National Alliance for Musical Theatre (NAMT): https://namt.org

- Edinburgh Fringe Festival: https://www.edfringe.com/

- Stratford Festival: https://www.stratfordfestival.ca/

Off-Off Broadway, Off-Broadway, and Broadway

Check out the following for audition information:

- Backstage: https://www.backstage.com/
- Playbill: http://www.playbill.com/
- Broadway World: https://www.broadwayworld.com/

Commercials, Voice-overs and Jingles

Television and radio commercials have many different kinds of work all rolled up into the finished product. You might be interested in being the on-camera talent, or you may be interested in narrating the commercial, or perhaps you want to be the one who sings the jingle—that catchy tune for the product. Or, maybe you have the skills to do all three. The more skills you develop, the more opportunities you give yourself for success.

If you've reached a point where you believe you have some solid acting experience and want to pursue work in television commercials, voice-overs or jingles, it's probably time to find an agent. Do an internet search to find a talent agency near you. An agent at one of these companies—and they usually have just one or two agents and an assistant in the smaller markets, might be interested in meeting you and taking you on as a client.

For an agent meeting, a simple resume and photo will be all you need. If an agent wants to work with you, they will want you to have a professional headshot and resume. The agent will advise you on your resume format and will have a list of reputable photographers for you to research and interview. Once you've had a photo session, the agent will be able to give you input on which photos to choose to be your "calling card." The agent will hear about auditions for television, film, and theater in your area and will send out your material (your picture and resume and maybe a video clip of something you've performed in) to the casting directors. If anyone is interested, they'll call your agent and give them an audition appointment to send to you. You'll likely get some "copy" or "sides" (a script of your lines) to learn before you go in to audition or you may be given the copy when you arrive.

Voice actors will be used to narrate—to voice-over—certain types of regular television commercials and do a wide variety of other types of work. Some of the types to explore are audiobooks, anime, cartoons, internet, radio, telephone prerecorded messages, looping (background for crowd scenes), and video game voice-over work. Are people always telling you have a great or distinctive voice? See if there's a voice-over class in your area where you can develop and hone some skills. Take some snippets of your best work in class and compile a demo to send out.

If you sing, you might want to do jingles. Jingles are catchy little tunes you hear running over or at the end of a television or radio commercial. The audition process will be the same as for on-camera work, you'll just be given music rather than copy.

Film

Student Films

If any of the local colleges or universities have film departments you can bet that there are students working on making their own movies. They have very little money, if any, and they need actors. Usually, they'll use acting majors at their schools. But every now and then they need a person of a "certain age" or a child or a guy who plays the accordion. Go to the school's website to look for audition notices or do an internet search for student film auditions. Keep an eye out on social media too for these types of posts. Sometimes you will be required to audition and sometimes the director might just ask if you can meet them for a cup of coffee after you've read the script.

Feature and Independent Films

Independents are small low-budget films usually being made by small production companies. Once the film is complete, they submit their finished product to film festivals and competitions with the hope that a legit studio will want to "distribute" it to movie theaters.

Big budget movies and independent films often shoot in small towns and need extras or local actors for roles that require just a few spoken lines. Be constantly looking for audition notices in all formats—newspapers, arts magazines, industry trade papers (publications specific to the arts) and of course the internet. If you have an agent, they will know about films being made locally and will submit you for them.

As I've said before, there's an information highway out there and there's really no question you cannot get an answer to if you find the right sources and know what questions to ask. Be diligent.

6 Curious Kids

What do you do when your child wants something this badly? Everything you can think of. I read Backstage religiously, talked to other parents, even made cold calls to agents and theaters. I believe it's a parent's sacred responsibility to show their children the world so they can find their place in it.

LENORE REIGEL, parent of child actors SAM REIGEL and EDEN REIGEL (both Emmy Award winners as adults), and award-winning film editor Tatiana S. Reigel, ACE

Once upon a time, there was a curious kid. They couldn't watch enough television or see enough movies. They never got tired of immersing themselves in other worlds. And to say that they were equally obsessed with plays and musicals would be an understatement. Take it from me, not only was I one of those kids but I now also coach and cast those kids and I can spot 'em a mile away.

Somehow, these kids recognize that there is a world of fun on the other side of the television, movie screen and up on the stage and they want to go play there. How they make that intellectual leap and then verbalize their wish to be a part of that other world is different for every kid. I met one of them on the very first national tour I ever did. There I was—an adult who finally had landed my first big job as a member of the ensemble of *Les Misérables*—and there was this kid—eight-year-old Andrew Harrison Leeds—who was playing the role of Gavroche and he *already* had a Broadway show credit on his resume. So how did he manage that? Here is his story in his own words:

My mom saw an advertisement in the newspaper that the Tampa Bay Performing Arts Center was looking for a kid to understudy the boys in a musical called Teddy & Alice. It was premiering in Tampa, Florida to work out the kinks before going to Broadway. I was 7 years old when I went to my "audition" for the local understudy position. I say "audition" in quotes because all I had to do was go into a room, with my mom, and talk to a woman named Laura. She liked my middle name—Harrison. And she liked how polite I was. And she gave me the job. I didn't have to act or sing for her. Strange, but that is what happened. I supposed they figured I'd never have to go on. And I never did go on. Near the end of the six-week run in Tampa, the crew started packing up. I sat with my mom backstage and I remember feeling sad. I turned to her and said, "I want to go to New York with them." My mom replied, "You should go ask Mrs. Shimberg if you can." Mrs. Shimberg was one of the producers and she happened to be standing at the end of the hallway. I remember being a little nervous maybe? But not too nervous. I really don't think I was concerned about being embarrassed if she said no. After all, what did I have to lose? I interrupted her talking to the stage manager, "Excuse me, Mrs. Shimberg. Do you think I could come to New York with you?" She said, "Do we even know if you can sing? Have you ever sung for us?" I answered honestly, "No." She told me to come to the orchestra pit at half hour so that she could hear me. At 7:30 I went down there with Mrs. Shimberg and the pianist and I sang Lambeth Walk from the musical Me and My Girl. I'm sure I was fine, but not spectacular. She told me to go back upstairs and wait. A few minutes later she arrived and informed me and my mother that I could continue on as the understudy in New York. And off we went! The show opened on Broadway to terrible reviews, but it did run long enough for the boy I was understudying to get released from his contract for misbehaving. And I got to take over the role. My life would be very different had I not walked down that hallway and asked Mrs. Shimberg if I could go to New York. As an adult, it's very hard to do something like that. There are too many fears, too many insecurities, too much awareness of how it might be perceived.

*But I often try to remind myself to forget about how much I now
know so that I might be brave enough to simply ask. Because it's
entirely possible the answer could be yes.*

And there you have it—just one of so many success stories on
ways to start out in the business. There are a million ways to seek
out opportunities for your child to participate and you will find
them now that you're aware your child is interested.

You can foster your child's curiosity by enrolling them in
classes and workshops while keeping an eye open for audition
opportunities. There are after-school programs for acting, singing,
dancing, television production, film editing, and playwriting.
There are acting classes for kids in your town and in every major
city. And there are summer camps (both day and sleepover)
and workshops at local community and regional theaters and
colleges. And they're for *all* ages. An online search for classes and
camps will turn up a variety of results no matter where you live.

It might be a good idea to start small to really find out if your kid
has been bitten by the "bug" before you spend money on the
tools of the trade. If it turns out that they are as crazy about the
arts as other kids may be about soccer or swimming or tennis
or skiing or any other sport or hobby, you'll know soon enough.

And while I'm all in favor of children finding their niches and
figuring out where they belong in this ever-changing world,
I'll just say to the parents and guardians of these extraordinary
kids who want to pursue their passions on a competitive
or professional level—do your best to make sure they stay
grounded. Above all, make sure they're allowed to be kids. And
also, make sure that if and when it doesn't seem like it's fun for
them anymore or becomes overwhelming or stressful in any
way—make sure they know they're allowed to stop doing it.

*Josh and I knew it was our job to keep Cory "a regular kid."
This meant regular activities during down time—trips to the*

park, bowling, etc. It also meant school remained important and academic expectations remained in place. We never said, "well because you're on Broadway . . . ." The show became a part of his life, but that is really the key, it was a part. We still had expectations of Cory as a member of our family, to be a good brother, participate when he could in family activities, try his best in school, and stay grounded with his friends. We tried to normalize things as best we could.

ERICA LEVENTHAL, parent of child actor CORY LOGAN,
School of Rock, *Broadway*

If a kid has a desire to be a professional actor and they are in a position to audition, they will soon know the despair of rejection. Guaranteed. Some will be able to shrug it off and keep going and others won't. It warrants careful monitoring to make sure they're okay. No matter how mature or talented or hard working they are, they are *not* adults and should not be treated as such.

As parents and guardians, you'll want to be well aware of the story your children are being asked to tell. Is there a sexual or romantic situation they will need to navigate? Are the lyrics in the song they choose to sing at the audition age-appropriate? That's all on you adults and it's really important to control those situations.

And again—the audition process is taxing and emotional enough for an adult but for kids and teenagers, it is *really* fraught, so it's a good idea to discuss the possibility of rejection, the lack of warmth or patience that they may feel in the audition room, or the fact that even though they may work hard to prepare material for an audition, they may not even be asked to perform any of it. The more you can help prepare them for those situations the better. Maybe prepare yourselves as best you can too. I've seen parents take these things much harder than their kids.

Beyond the kids' physical, mental and emotional health, with children there are issues and industry needs that very often speak to their *cast-ability* that adults do not face. Children aren't fully formed in mind or body. Far from it. The process of auditioning and casting children—while the same for adults in many ways—is always much more involved, depending the child's age.

For example, in the musical *Miss Saigon*, there is a character named Tam which is played by a very young child. They do not speak and they do not sing. However, they are required to crawl in and out of dark spaces, and remain extremely quiet, and still while on stage except when they are asked to color in a coloring book. Do you know how hard it is to tell a four-year-old child to sit still and color and ignore everything going on around them but at the same time to listen for their cue to run and jump into their "mother's" arms when they hear it? When auditioning *Tams*, we play games to help us gauge the child's listening skills and to see their physical agility. There are loud gunshots in the show, so in order to test how the kids will react, we give them earplugs to muffle the sound and we shoot off the prop gun. Then we take the earplugs out and shoot the gun off again. We work our way up as best we can until we are simulating the moment the gun is shot on stage in performance. Beyond the surprise of the sound and volume of the gunshot itself, the child will also watch the other actors feign hurt and dying and see their clothes (costumes) seeped with (fake) blood. These are all potentially traumatizing situations—must the kids be so young? In this case it's necessary because they need to be small enough for the young woman playing "Kim," who is often very teeny herself, to pick them up, carry and hold them while running, singing, etc.

Under normal circumstances—we are in a room and the child will come in alone or with their "adult" if they'd prefer. Often, we'll bring the kids into the room in a group and play games and work with them together before seeing them alone. In group auditions for very young children, such as the one for *Miss Saigon*, we have the parents and guardians sit in the child's line of sight which usually makes them feel safe while they work with the creative team, who are strangers to them. This allows the parents to witness the process and to understand the working environment their children will be living in if they are cast. This is important because once the kid is hired, the parent must turn over custody of the child actor to an at-work guardian for each performance. The audition process is actually a very valuable tool in gauging the all-important level of independence of the child.

As we audition kids who are a little older, the conversation changes to discussing elements like timelines. "Well, he's great now but there's a chance his voice will change by the time we get to opening night. Let's go with the younger kid." Or, "Love her but her Mom said she's grown three inches in the last year. If she gets any taller, she'll tower over the other kids and it'll be hard to believe she's the youngest . . .," and so it goes throughout all the age ranges until adulthood.

If you are really serious about pursuing a career for your child in the professional field of acting, you'll have many of the same questions asked by all aspiring actors, plus a few more that are child specific. For instance, there are child labor laws that cover their safety, health and well-being while at work. Kids can only work a certain number of hours in any given day and if they must miss school the producers must hire an accredited tutor to work with them.

But in general, the questions about starting a career are the same—how to get into the business and what are the tools of the trade.

First, you'll need a picture and a resume. The picture part is easy. You can do this yourself to start but eventually you'll need to go to a photographer and have some professional shots taken. Do an internet search for actor headshots to see what's on trend and explore your options. I think a three-quarter shot (from above the knees or waist) is preferable because it tends to have a less posed, more candid feel. Plus, it just gives us more information. But that's a matter of taste and it's not mandatory. The most important thing about a headshot is that they be a good representation of what the child actor currently looks like. In real life. So, for kids especially, it means keeping it real— makeup and hair styling are optional and should always look natural. Once you have a good photo, make 8 × 10 inch sized prints. Staple the resume back-to-back to the photo. You'll need to trim the resume to the same size as the 8 × 10 inch photo.

You'll need a resume that is representative of your kid's work. At the beginning, there may be no credits. That's okay. At the top, print your child's name, *your* phone number, *your* email address (create one for business stuff), and your name and relationship to the actor. You'll list their date of birth (DOB) and their current height. Please keep the height up to date. You can have a training section listing where they're taking classes or workshops. If they have performed in anything, list the role and production information. You'll always want to carry a few of these around if you're heading to in-person auditions. Keep a digital copy up to date so it's always ready to be emailed at a moment's notice. You never know when you'll need one.

If your child wants to be a pro, you may wonder if you need an agent and how to go about getting one.

> For us having a manager and agents has helped us stay Mom and Dad. It's important for us that Julian can talk about work options with his manager and make decisions and then be able to go to his parents and talk with us separately. We let him know that we support him 100 percent and give advice when he asks for it. Julian LOVES acting and performing so it truly is all fun for

him. It is so special for Dan and I to watch our child thrive and pursue his passion with such happiness.

ERIN BELLARD, *parent of child actor* JULIAN LERNER, Les Misérables, *national tour,* The Wonder Years, *television.*

You certainly don't need an agent or manager in the beginning—you can audition on your own for the community theater or for a school play—but you may soon reach a time when you want some expertise and guidance on seeking work in more professional realms.

Depending on where you live and how far you are willing to travel for jobs as well as auditions, you'll want to do an internet search for talent agencies that have a department for child actors—a youth department. Even if you live in a small city or town there's bound to be at least one or two talent agencies not too far away. All of them have websites which will give information on how to go about sending them your child's picture and resume for perusal as a possible new client. Be sure to do your research on them. Look at their histories and client lists and make sure they are "legit" (licensed and franchised). It's those agents who will know how to submit your child for more professional work and how to move your kid's career forward.

My career as a casting director has been very much about finding and casting children. I have cast the Broadway and Touring companies of *Les Misérables*, *Miss Saigon* and *School of Rock*. Off-Broadway, I cast *Trevor The Musical*. Regionally I have cast *Last Days of Summer* and *A Walk on the Moon*. I've helped cast kids for sketches on *The Tonight Show* and *Saturday Night Live*. All of these varied productions had different requirements. They needed children ranging in age from four to seventeen with skills such as singing, acting, dancing, reciting poetry, basketball dribbling, jumping rope, guitar playing, stand-up comedy and gymnastics. Doing stand-up comedy *while* doing gymnastics . . . okay, not really, but you get the picture.

Every kid is different and what the creative teams respond positively to will also be different. But there is one thing that is exactly the same for all the projects I've ever cast—film, television, theater, across the board. Everyone says, "We need kids who aren't 'show-biz-y.'" What we mean by "show-biz-y" is a child who is trying so hard to perform that they can't seem to be themselves in the audition room and there's truly nothing worse than that.

Of course, we always want kids to demonstrate a level of politeness and the desire to be there, but I've seen kids lose jobs because their parents coach them into a state of fear about how they should conduct themselves during the audition. As a result, the work becomes incredibly "perform-y." It's not natural, genuine or authentic. Now we have to be real here, too, because we know kids tend to learn things by rote. But it's great when we know they are capable of making adjustments in their performance and if they are so over-rehearsed and their audition is so planned out that they can't do something different on the spot, it will concern us.

Rehearsal is the process for getting to the performance. But the audition comes first, and *auditioning* is all about the kids showing who they are in that moment with the material they've been asked to prepare. While we need to know they are capable of memorizing and taking acting notes and have at least made a choice or two about the work they'll do in the audition room, no one is looking for anything too polished. We want kids who feel like kids—sometimes messy, sometimes moody, sometimes unsure of themselves. That's not only ok, it is good. It's preferred. It's necessary. And I promise that's not anything you can manufacture except by encouraging your child to be themselves and have fun with the audition and the rehearsal process.

Part 2
The Tools of
the Trade

7 Pictures, Resumes, Reels, and Websites

Sending out pictures and resumes should be reserved for submitting on specific shows to specific people in order for that to be most effective. Pictures and resumes sent to an office just generally—"Please consider me for anything your office is working on . . ." is useless and they will wind up unopened in the recycling bin. Be selective with your mailings and save the 8 × 10s for very specific submissions, making sure to address per project per point person and then follow-up with postcards that have your picture and contact info on them.

Keep the follow-up going! Follow-up, by the way, asks nothing of the recipient. It should be clear you know they have no obligation to respond. Following up is strictly about doing what you can to keep yourself at the forefront of the minds of casting directors, nothing more.

Pictures

These, along with your resumes, are your calling cards. We look at these photos and believe what we see and it takes a *long time*, if ever—for that first impression to change, so you have to get these pictures *right*. First and foremost—they need to *look like the person who walks through the door* at the audition. We need as much *truth* in these pictures as we hope to get from your acting.

How do we get as much information about you as possible from your photos? Well, hopefully we see as much personality as possible—a certain pose, a light in your eyes that gives me an idea of who you are. Search the internet with the keywords headshots for actors and see what the trends are and which photographers' work you're drawn to.

If I carve out some time to see actors I've never met before, I am doing so based on what I see in their photo and read on their resume, so it'd be nice if what I've seen there is actually what I get when I meet them.

We know that sometimes you wear more or less makeup, and that sometimes you change your hair color or hairstyle, and that you need photos that represent a couple of different looks, but please be sure all those different looks still look like *you*. And while it's all well and good to have hair and makeup geniuses at your photo shoots, when you show up in person, you need to look as close to your pictures as possible, so you should be able to replicate those different looks on your own.

Resumes

There are so many dos and don'ts! Except . . . there *aren't*.

There is no one format that is a *must* except that your resume needs to be legible. And easy to decipher. That's it.

Your resume should represent the highlights (and I *do* mean the highlights—not everything you've ever done) of your work.

We know you have to start somewhere. We also know—and you should also be aware—that the roles you played in camp or college are probably not realistic as far as what you're going to be right for in the professional arena. But don't lie or pad or overemphasize—just tell us what you've been doing and be selective about it. As far as roles, just because you *can* (or *have*) doesn't mean you *will* (or *should*) continue on in that vein.

That said—maybe what's important about a given credit is the director you got to work with, or the fact that the show is known to be challenging vocally, or that you did a season somewhere where you successfully did ten shows in ten days . . . *this* is useful information. It tells us about your skill levels and how people *who've cast you* view you.

Remember that all your resume tells us is that somewhere, at some time, someone thought highly enough of you to hire you. People get cast for many reasons. It doesn't tell me whether you were any good or not, so I'm starting fresh in the audition room. Like your photos, the resumes are just a jumping-off point—but an important one because usually—if it's truly representative of who you are as an actor—it'll be what helps to get you in the door in the first place.

Personal Stats on Your Resumes

Height = yes. We need this information, and not only for children and dancers. We have to factor in height because the director has told us their vision for the *look* of the piece, the *silhouette*, the big picture. Of course we try to think outside the box and take risks with our choices—just like you do as an actor, but we do have an obligation, especially having been told in no uncertain terms what the team is looking for—to make sure you fit, quite literally, into that picture, so please tell the truth.

Weight = no. Too many people have preconceived notions about actual numbers. Your picture should tell us what we need to know for a start.

Home address = no. For obvious reasons.

Email and phone number and website address = yes. For obvious reasons.

A note about your email address and online identity: in this business, *you* are the brand and *your name* is the brand name. Your choice of a professional name should be suited to your business model, so it's worth some serious consideration.

You will want to check with all the professional unions and domain registration websites to see if your name is taken. If it's in use, find a variation that works for you. It's an internet world and you want your name, your brand, to be the same across all media platforms and unions. You will want to keep your personal email separate from your professional one.

And not for nothing—think of the visceral feeling you get when you see an email address for the first time. Do you really want someone who is or will hopefully become a potential professional business resource to be writing to you at (and mentally identifying or categorizing you as) "partygirl21@ hotmail.com"? Trust me, you don't.

Film and Television Extra Work

While it's not a bad idea as an income-producing day job and you really can learn a lot if you pay attention, listing jobs as an extra on your resume is not advised.

Special Skills on the Resume

These are a constant source of amusement for creative teams so please be careful and professional. The special skills you list should show value for potential jobs, be they in theater, TV, film or commercials. If you choose to list a whimsical skill, do so at your own peril.

The idea that if you put silly, cool stuff in your special skills section it might open up a conversation with the people behind the table, thus getting you a little more time in the room—that's a myth. If you do include a quirky special skill, you had better be ready to show us then and there that you actually can recite all of the State capitals backward in alphabetical order. Just think about how you'd handle a resume for a job other than acting and do that.

Reels

Anyone can have a reel these days and everyone should. These don't need to be fancy; they simply need to show your work.

If you don't yet have any professional clips, create your own. Rent a studio, get someone to video you doing two contrasting monologues, and if you sing—two contrasting songs. Dance reels that include several different styles, including tumbling if you do that, are helpful for musical theater. Include your reel on your website and make sure you use a format that can be easily opened and viewed. This self-produced work can be added to a video you may already have of a commercial, television show, or film that you've done. There's no need to worry about spending a lot of money on production value—all that matters is that the sound and picture are clear.

The purpose of the reel is to give casting directors, agents, and creative teams a tool to help them see your work. Reels give you a leg up, so be sure they're posted and easy to find on every media platform available to you.

Websites

A website is a very important part of your tool kit. We do almost all of our research online. If you do not have an agent or manager, we still need to be able to find you. We *will* go looking for you via all online resources.

Casting directors almost never have a creative team who will all be familiar with every actor's body of work—after all, that's our job—and it is up to us to educate the team. Along with lists of names, we send corresponding pictures and resumes and—here's the gist—when it is available—a link to the actor's website or reel. If you don't have an online presence—you're less likely to be seriously considered.

If I can direct the creative team to your website or reel where they can view samples of your work it's a great way for them to e-meet you and learn about your skills. That's what helps you with true consideration and gives you a shot when we are not seeing people in person. Let's say we are casting a reading and there won't be any auditions because there is no money yet to pay for them (auditions cost money—studios, accompanists, readers, copies of sides and music). However, often during the developmental process—a casting director will be brought on (usually for a free lunch and a dollar just the same as the actors).

You must exist and be easy to find in the online world. Create content if you don't have any. Make sure all the links work and that the site is easy to open on any phone or tablet or computer. It doesn't have to be expensive; it just needs to be easy to navigate and a good representation of your work.

8 Representation and Submissions

Agents and managers are there to represent *you*. You want someone in your corner who will protect your interests and help you to see and to define your future in the acting profession. While it's a business, and they take you on as a client because they see you and your skill set as a viable commodity—your relationship with them is personal, so if you don't feel that they have your best interests at heart, then they are not for you. Literally—they are not *for* you. Having a solid working relationship with your representation is a critical part of your business, so do everything you can to find a good fit.

Both *can* submit you for jobs and *should*. When you do have both, it's important that they have a good working relationship with each other, as well.

That an actor has representation tells me nothing more than just that—they have representation. This fact doesn't make me think that an actor is more talented or more viable than an unrepresented actor. And here's a little encouragement to back that up:

> I would definitely take a chance on someone with few or no professional credits depending on the role and how well the person does during the audition process. Sometimes experience does come into play because of the requirements of a role. But if they feel right for the role, I'd trust my gut and I would absolutely take a chance.

CASEY NICHOLAW, Tony Award-winning Director, The Book of Mormon; Tony Award Best Director nominations for Drowsy Chaperone, Something Rotten, Mean Girls and The Prom; Tony Award Best Choreographer nominations for Spamalot, Drowsy Chaperone, Book of Mormon, Aladdin, Something Rotten and Mean Girls.

I will often take a chance on an actor with few credits. Rarely do I look at their resume before the audition. I judge them on their talent in the room without any preconceived notions.

SUSAN STROMAN, Tony Award-winning Director and Choreographer, The Producers; Tony Award-winning Choreographer, Crazy For You, Show Boat and Contact; Tony Award Best Director Nominations, Contact, The Music Man and The Scottsboro Boys; Tony Award Best Choreographer Nominations, Big, Steel Pier, The Music Man, Oklahoma!, The Scottsboro Boys and Bullets Over Broadway.

Agents and Managers

First off, let's dispel the notion that you can stop doing the work when you have an agent, that you can just sit back and wait for them to call you with an appointment. You must always be your own best advocate. Never stop being proactive. I can't emphasize this enough—you're equally responsible. You're your own full-time job. You are your *only* client and they have *many* others.

The agent usually does the submitting, unless you *only* have a manager. The agent takes the audition appointment, gets you your audition materials, and passes along notes to you from the casting director or perhaps from someone else on the creative team.

If you have both an agent and a manager, then the manager will become involved when it comes time to go to contract—to negotiate. If you do not have a manager, the agent will negotiate your contract. When you have both, they will often partner to negotiate.

If you have a manager and not an agent—or vice-versa, either one is perfectly capable of undertaking all of those tasks on your behalf.

The addition of a manager usually doesn't happen until your career warrants it. For example, you are a regular on a television show, you're working on a film while on hiatus from the show and hosting a charity event. As you become more in demand, you'll find yourself in need of more support to help manage things like personal appearances, concerts, a few days you might need off because you have family obligations. Or a manager may be interested in taking you on as a developmental client in order to help you build your career from the ground up. Depending on where you are in your career, you may also have an attorney or a business manager and they, too, may be involved, along with your agent and/or manager, in the deal-making.

Whether you have an agent or a manager, or both, your representation should have access to the *breakdowns* (information about the projects and the character descriptions currently being sought). If they don't have access, it may mean they are not franchised (have not yet entered into an affiliate agreement with the entertainment industry unions). If they're not, it might simply mean that they are a new agency and have recently opened up shop—but it is worth asking why they aren't, and when they will be, franchised.

Submissions

When you are *submitted*, it means your picture and resume are being sent to the casting director. This can be done electronically or via snail mail. If you have an agent or manager, they will frequently do this (versus you "self" submitting) and then follow up with the casting director and fight for you to be seen for the role in question.

In order for agents or managers to do their jobs effectively, they must have a strong, positive relationship with the casting folks. They need to be trusted by the casting directors. They earn that trust by repeatedly sending talented actors who are truly right for the needs of the role. They have a successful track record. They are colleagues with the casting directors and each works to do what truly serves the actor and the project best.

When an agent calls to fight for two or three of their clients and I know they've done their homework—whether that means they've seen this particular long-running show or that they've asked me to educate them on what I'm really looking for in this moment, I'm grateful. I *need* the agents and managers to educate me about you as well. And remember, with or without an agent, that's still *your* job, too—to educate me about you.

I've cast *many* actors without representation who are just as talented as the actors with powerhouse agencies. That said, it benefits you to have an agent because hopefully they will be privy to information that you may not have because of their carefully cultivated industry relationships and their access to breakdown services. And they truly have the ears of the casting directors who likewise have the trust of the creative team—because they've *earned* that trust.

Please don't become one of the many actors who get lazy once they have representation. Those are the actors who stop attending open calls and the Equity auditions. They stop submitting themselves for student and independent films—all the things you can and should continue to do on your own. They sit back and they wait for their agents to call with an appointment. But unless you've got an appointment—you need to *show up* at those open calls. Unless and until you have multiple Broadway shows under your belt and are a well-known entity in film and television, you need to continue to do the work of putting yourself out there.

Even if your agency is small and has only five clients, when your agent wakes up in the morning, they've got more on their minds than just you. Again, and it bears repeating, *you* are your *only* client.

Remember that your representative works with you and *for* you. While you need and want them—this needs to be a balanced relationship. You can't feel afraid to call the office. You need to have a game plan with them and be secure in the knowledge that you both are working toward the same goals and fighting for the same thing—you.

You must agree on the kinds of roles and jobs to pursue and above all, you must feel comfortable communicating with each other. If you cannot do that there is something wrong. Sometimes when an actor starts to falter and is not getting auditions, I suggest that it might be time for a meaningful conversation with their agent to ask what they can do to increase the chance of getting seen. Ask if you are in agreement as far as how you both see yourself and the types of roles you should be submitted for. *Important*— this is best done in person and needs to be done with courtesy and respect and an attitude toward problem-solving. If you are accusatory and angry, you'll be digging a hole for yourself out of which you'll never be able to climb.

That said, if you have an agent or manager but you're not happy with them, as long as you don't feel they are leading you astray or behaving in a way you cannot tolerate, stick with them, even while you look elsewhere. And if you feel you must part ways, always try to end the relationship as gracefully as possible. Avoid burning bridges.

I have relationships with the powerhouse agents and managers who take care of award-winning actors and big box-office draws. I need them for obvious reasons, but I also treasure my connections with the smaller houses—the ones nurturing new talent. Makes sense, right?

But no matter what level you're on—you always need to do your part in forming relationships with anyone and everyone who can help get you in the audition room!

Getting Meetings with Potential Representation

Ask everyone you know about their agencies. Maybe one is a good fit for you. You might want to steer clear of asking people who are similar to you type-wise for agent recommendations though. Talk to actors older than you or who are completely different types so that you won't appear to be in competition with them. Always be sure to ask them if they'd feel comfortable putting you in touch with their agent.

Do your research. Look at agent websites—educate yourselves on their client lists—submit yourself to those who would be a good fit for you via those websites.

Take classes and workshops and attend panels featuring agents and managers in the business and pursue the ones who seem like the best fit for you.

As you look for representation, don't forget you can self-submit to casting directors. Slip your picture and resume under the door at their offices. Do not knock or ring the bell. If there are no mail slots, just leave your materials outside the door. Or call the office and get an email address so you can electronically submit for a specific project. Note: it is not advised, and actually kind of a no-no, to call casting offices, but if you are succinct, quick, and specific, "Hi, I'd like to self-submit for *All's Well That Ends Well* at the Old Globe. Are you able to tell me to whom the submission should be addressed?"—that'll serve you best. But please only do that if you've tried every other avenue available to you. Try Playbill.com, Equity online, Backstage.com—you can get a lot of information from a variety of trade publications. Use your resources and confirm your information. The assistants (answerers of phones and the all-important gatekeepers at any casting office) usually know all there is to know about their office's projects—how far along in the audition process they are, if there are offers out on any roles yet, when the callbacks will take place, if you should use a British accent or be able to do a triple time step. Those assistants can be a valuable resource, so always be at your professional best when dealing with them.

At all costs—make sure you submit to a specific person or at the very least on a specific project. And it bears repeating, lose the cover letters—if what you have to say can't fit on a sticky note, then you're saying too much.

Continue to do all of this even if you have an agent and a manager!

At the end of the day, this is all relentlessly hard work but work begets work. It makes you better at your craft. And it's why so often the people who work harder, but may be less talented, often get the job. If you stop working, somebody somewhere will be waiting in the wings to seize your missed opportunity. It is rigorous and exhausting and you'll need to stay healthy and keep your skills sharp in order to compete effectively at the professional level.

9 Unions

When It's Time to Join

A most memorable challenge came my way when I won an apprenticeship at the prestigious Burt Reynolds Institute for Theater Training (BRITT). At that time, Burt Reynolds was one of the biggest box-office stars in movie history. He had a very successful dinner theater in Jupiter, Florida, where all his famous pals went to direct and act in plays. He founded an apprentice program to work in conjunction with his theater. For those lucky few chosen to be in the program, at the end of the yearlong apprenticeship, the ever-elusive Actor's Equity Card was the prize. I auditioned twice for the program. Twice I was not chosen. But I was waitlisted the second time and I got lucky. Someone dropped out and I was in.

I apprenticed for a solid year for practically no salary. I sewed sequins onto costumes for Bob Fosse's *Dancin'* until I went blind. I took a bucket and a mop and every night at intermission I washed down the entire set of *Orphans*. I performed throughout the local community in fundraisers. We also had duties in the many shows at the dinner theater itself. I understudied multiple roles and simultaneously served as a dresser for other actors in those very same shows. I understudied Marilyn McCoo (lead singer of the Grammy award-winning group the Fifth Dimension) and Beth Fowler (leading lady of Broadway) in *A . . . My Name is Alice*. I went on unexpectedly one night for Ms. McCoo, fell from a platform in a blackout, and broke all my ribs. I was laid up for two solid weeks—taking a breather was never so painful.

It was a truly grueling and amazing year. I made life-long friends and learned that no task was beneath me. We were overworked, underpaid and about as happy as we could be. I wish that experience for everyone.

I took my Equity card at the end of that year because I was ready to play on the next level. But I was ready because I'd spent a few years playing roles in non-Equity theater. That's what I'd made sacrifices for to begin with—to be there doing that coveted apprenticeship. I was ready.

That said, make no mistake, it got harder, not easier, to book jobs. Because after I joined Equity, I was playing in an arena with more experienced people and the competition was, without a doubt, more daunting.

And guess what? I didn't work as much. Often an actor who finds himself in that situation will take a temporary leave from Equity so they can go do non-Equity work—because they want to, and have to, work. It's a slippery slope, though, and I highly recommend staying union once you've made the hard-earned leap. Suck it up and keep going.

This is all to say that joining a union warrants a lot of thought. That is yet another moment when you'll want to ask yourself all those tough questions—about what's important to *you*— and answer them thoughtfully and truthfully. Remember, it's a marathon, not a sprint. Try not to think of it as a competition. It's all about you, your personal best, and where you set the finish line. And what's good and right for *you* is not the same as what's best for your colleagues.

I've found that, as with anything in the professional world, we learn what we need to know when we need to know it in order to protect ourselves. So here we'll just talk about what *I think you should consider* regarding when it's time to join the various unions—then you should get the union rules books and take each thing as it comes.

Actors Equity Association—The Union for Stage Actors

Should I join Equity? If so, when? What are the pros and cons? This seems like it should be an easy yes. If you have the chance to join Equity, do! But it's not that black and white.

There are a few different ways to work your way into Equity. For instance, let's say you show up at an Equity call, get seen, and after the audition process, get cast. That's fantastic, but now, the thing is, you have to join in order to accept that job. Or, you can apprentice or intern at places which allow you to accrue enough 'points' to join. At that point, you are an Equity Membership Candidate (EMC) and are eligible to join. Alternatively, Equity membership is open to any actor who has worked professionally on a theater production in the United States, even if that theater was a non-Equity production. You will need to provide proof of that work and proof of *payment* for that work (e.g., pay stub, W2, 1099, etc.). Your application and a $600 down payment toward the initiation fee are required. This may change in years to come, as this last way to join came about as a direct result of the theater shut down in 2020, but you can always check the current rules.

https://actorsequity.org/join/openaccess/.

Joining Equity is simple once you are eligible. But 'to join or not to join' is the question.

Reasons *not* to join: there are so many more opportunities in the NON-EQ world. You will more likely be considered for a principal role in the NON-EQ world and that experience makes you better. It adds credits to your resume and makes you more prepared later, when you do join, to actually compete at that level. You'll hone your craft at these NON-EQ jobs. By the time you've earned your eligibility, or decided to just join up, you'll have some solid experience and some good credits on your resume, so my advice is to get your card when you feel ready.

It's the Equity jobs that actually start to let you pay your rent, accrue weeks of work toward eligibility for health care benefits, and receive pension contributions from the producer. Go for it! If you go for it, you'll learn a lot and grow as an artist. Just my opinion.

Being a union member has its advantages to be sure—as I've already stated. But as far as auditions are concerned, it doesn't give you any advantages with casting directors beyond the fact that you'll have more access to and more knowledge about projects because as a union member you'll have more resources available to you. It doesn't affect my opinion of your work if you don't have your Equity card when you audition for me— it simply means that if hired to be employed under an Equity contract, you must join in order to be able to do the job.

I get asked all the time if it matters to me—if my opinions about an actor's talents, are influenced by whether they belong to Equity. Nope. The only thing I know for sure is that somehow you fit the bill and got hired for an Equity show. Or, you did that third apprenticeship that finally resulted in your eligibility. Or you worked enough non-Equity gigs, paid your initiation fees and first dues, and you're in.

But remember, while they may bring more experience, someone who belongs to Actors Equity isn't necessarily more talented or impressive or more right for any given job than someone who's not a member.

Screen Actors Guild-American Federation of Television and Radio Artists (SAG-AFTRA) for Film, Television and Voice Actors

Now it's different with SAG-AFTRA. If I want to hire a non-SAG-AFTRA actor on a union SAG-AFTRA show or film, I have to prove to SAG-AFTRA that I have searched high and low for a union actor and I simply cannot find one with the particular skill set I need.

In addition—it often takes a while to get an approval from SAG-AFTRA to hire a non-union actor—and the job may come and go before approval arrives. If I go ahead and hire that non-union actor and it later comes back that SAG-AFTRA has ruled against my request, the production will be fined. This does not bode well for me, the casting director, because my decision resulted in an unnecessary cost to the production.

We would be likely to take a chance and hire someone non-union without timely approval from the unions in pretty much only one situation: the producers would all need to be reasonably certain that approval was forthcoming or they'd want this person so badly that they'd be willing to pay any fines that might be incurred. That is likely to be the case if they needed a guy who could ride a motorcycle while juggling knives and who speaks Russian. Since that population's relatively small (and if I find that guy, he may not even be an actor), producers will likely take the chance and hire him.

And here's another nugget: you do not need to join SAG-AFTRA the first time you're hired to work on a union set. If you are offered a *speaking* role, and that's a first for you, you can be either Taft-Hartley'd (Taft Hartley is the Labor Management Relations act of 1947 which, in this case, gives you a pass to work *one gig and one gig only* without being a union member), or join the union at that time. You might choose not to join for that first job because you can't afford the dues just yet. To summarize, after accepting that first speaking role in a film or a TV show, if you are Taft-Hartley'd the first time, the *next time* you are offered a job on a SAG-AFTRA set—you *must* join in order to work.

10 Networking

Networking is necessary. It must be done. And it comes in the most surprising forms. Networking covers a broad spectrum of interactions within the business community. Every bit of work you do, and how you present yourself as a human being, in *any and every* situation in this business, counts.

It was in fact networking that ultimately led me to this career I so love. During the time in my life when I was struggling to find my way as an actor, a friend who was producing a sitcom came to me and mentioned that the casting company working on his show was looking for an assistant. He knew I'd been feeling pretty lost and wondered if this was something I might want to look into. I interviewed for that job and I promptly became the oldest living assistant to a casting director on the planet. I fetched food and cut sides for bosses who were, in many instances, ten years younger than me. Humbling. But I found that I am a person who likes a steady paycheck. Plus, I was getting it—the casting thing. Ironically, I think it was partially my maturity that ultimately helped me move up fairly quickly—I knew to keep my mouth shut and my eyes and my ears open. I was promoted. I learned how it worked in TV and film—not only about the audition process in that arena but also about the contracts and the politicking of it all.

And so there ensued a series of timely events that brought me to the casting department at Dreamworks Studios and ultimately to ABC Television. Suffice it to say, an office overlooking the Hollywood sign and a car that didn't embarrass me at the valet—plus getting to work with some really creative and groundbreaking people did *not* suck.

Now, I realize a lot of people hate networking. Networking has a bad rap because it makes people feel needy and undignified but it's always about *your approach*. If you're someone who is truly uncomfortable with networking, try to shift your way of thinking. Try to make peace with it and have some fun.

Consider the following scenario. One day you bump into a famous producer/director—let's call her "Jane Smith"—in an elevator. You say hello and tell her you're an admirer, and thank her for her work. When you get off that elevator, you immediately let your agent know about that encounter, because, coincidentally, you've been trying to get an audition for "Jane Smith's" new project. Now your agent has a little story to pass on to the casting director when pushing to get you seen.

If you don't have an agent, you pull out your postcard (with your picture and contact info) and drop a note to the casting director saying, "Hi. Hope you're well! I bumped into 'Jane Smith' today and it reminded me to be in touch to say I hope you'll keep me in mind when setting up appointments for her new project." As a casting director, I may or may not set you up for an appointment for this show, but what I might do is bring you in for something else, which I may not have thought to do, had you not gotten in touch.

And there you have it—a perfect example of networking that was not needy, undignified or uncomfortable for any of the parties involved.

I often find myself looking back at how things started—what series of events led me to any given point. Someone asks, "How'd you two meet?" or "Where do you know them from?" and *almost always* the answer is from being active in the community—through an audition or a job, from behind the table or in front of the table, in the waiting room, or, just as often, through an introduction by a friend or a friend of a friend or a colleague.

Networking comes naturally when you fully immerse yourself in the community. You do this by following up on chance meetings with directors in elevators, by getting off your couch and going to see plays and going for a drink afterward. You do this by saying hello to your friends backstage after you see their show, by taking classes and keeping an ear to the ground about who's doing what and when and where, and by joining in the conversation.

Often, it's because you said something kind, or did great work, or because you put yourself out for someone, that you'll be remembered well. Just when you think you didn't make a good impression or that you were dismissed or forgotten— something positive and hopeful will happen that can be traced back to groundwork you unknowingly laid two years ago. As a casting director, I'm the poster child for bringing in actors to audition because I first saw them at a different audition two or four or six years ago. It's our job to keep people who impress us on our radar. Networking *works*.

That all said, when you're out and about and you cross paths with industry professionals, please do *not* ask to get together for a quick cup of coffee so that you can pick their brains about the business. Please don't mistake this type of interaction for networking. While we genuinely want to help—there is no such thing as a quick coffee or lunch. People are *busy* and they also hate having to say no because most people are kind. The better thing to do is ask if they would mind if you emailed them with a couple of questions. If they are open to that, then fire off a *short* note with one or two specific and succinct questions. One or two solved mysteries are better than none. And you can go to different people for advice on different topics tailored to them so you don't wind up asking too much of any one person.

One of the very specific questions you might ask someone in casting is how they'd like you to keep in touch. You'll likely get a different answer from every one of them but your attention to their needs will pay off.

If you send me a picture and resume or a note or a postcard—if you mention the project in which you are interested and your self-submission has my name on it, it will make its way to my desk and it will get opened and looked at. This may not happen in as timely a fashion as you'd like, but it will happen. I speak only for myself here but let's face it, even if nothing comes of that self-submission, you've at least reminded me you exist and have given yourself a shot.

But for following up and keeping in touch, I like a postcard. Not the "Vienna is beautiful, wish you were here!" kind of postcard but the one you have professionally printed that has your photo and contact information on one side and room for a note on the other.

Postcards have many purposes. Maybe you want to invite me to something. Or maybe you want me to bring you in to audition for a show you're hearing about or maybe you just want to remind me of your existence—doesn't matter. Stay in touch.

If I get a postcard from you every six weeks then it usually goes like this: "Oh yea!"—I think, pulling up the memory of you—(toss it in recycling). Six weeks later another postcard arrives: "Oh yeah!" (toss it in recycling). Six weeks after that—same. I don't feel guilty about this because postcards are cheap and so is the postage. Then one day your postcard arrives (and by now I cannot help but know who you are because you've been diligent!), *and* the timing is right and I think, "Oh yeah! Glad this came today, because *now* I have something coming up that I want to explore this person for." Yay! See how that works? And by the way, please always make a note reminding me (*every time*—even years after our first meeting) where and how we met. There are so many of you and only one of me, so help me to remember, okay?

These are just a few examples of how to be memorable, how to form relationships, and how to stay in the forefront of peoples' minds. Let me reiterate that every casting director will have a different way that they'll want you to keep in touch. When you have the chance, ask people what they prefer. Make a note so you'll remember their preference and be able to accommodate them. Just keep networking!

11 Continuing Education

I have friends who are Tony, Emmy, and/or Golden Globe nominees and winners. Almost all of them still take class, teach when they can, and still work with a coach before their own auditions. Each thinks they will never work again. I am of the belief that it is because they never stop learning and perfecting their craft and they get better as a result, that they do indeed keep getting acting jobs.

Maybe you've just graduated from college or you've been earning a living for years as an actor. You *must* continue to hone your craft. You must always be learning. I learn something new every time I teach a class or coach an actor.

Whether you commit to a beginning tap class or you take a playwriting course or you start a yoga practice—being in class not only helps develop discipline but it also ensures that you're constantly meeting new people. Someone will know something that'll be useful to you in some way. You'll listen to people talk. You'll hear of a new series that is looking for people who speak Hebrew and can ride a unicycle. Hey, you can do both those things! You wouldn't have known about that if you had stayed home, if you had not been out and participating (networking) and being a contributing member of society.

You'll become better actors because you're immersing yourself always with people who are studying and pursuing their goals and trying to better themselves.

Those are the environments where you test out new audition material, learn that time step (even if it's the only thing you master as a dancer!), build your audition song books, try and fail, and come out better.

Continuing education doesn't have to cost a ton of cash—here are just a few examples:

- Read a book—any book. Start with the history of acting.
- Study new-to-you acting methods. Delve into those that you aren't familiar with.
- Go to the Lincoln Center Library for the Performing Arts in New York City or the Museum of Television and Radio in Los Angeles and watch a Broadway show or an episode of a classic television show there.
- Watch all the television shows or movies by a particular director or from a certain era.
- Study a genre for a little while. Watch every Alfred Hitchcock film, watch a curated collection of silent or foreign films. Watch every Three Stooges film. Binge watch old Bugs Bunny cartoons and then compare them to the film "Who Framed Roger Rabbit?" (Just throwing out a few ideas here that'll help you understand.)
- Find and watch documentaries on the entertainment industry.

If you need a place to start, here's some recommended reading and viewing:

Books:

Sanford Meisner: On Acting, Sanford Meisner

Respect for Acting, Uta Hagen

Easy Riders, Raging Bulls: How the Sex-Drugs-and-Rock 'N' Roll Generation Saved Hollywood, Peter Biskind (both movies—Easy Rider and Raging Bull should also be watched!)

An Actor Prepares, Constantin Stanislavski

Real Life Drama: The Group Theatre and America 1931–1940, Wendy Smith

Act One, Moss Hart

Next Season: A Novel, Michael Blakemore

History of the Theatre, Brockett and Hildy

The Actor and the Target, Declan Donnellan

The Empty Space, Peter Brook

Plays:

I'll do this by playwright. You should really be at least a little familiar with their work. Google their most famous works if you need a place to start.

Edward Albee

Anton Checkhov

Noel Coward

Christopher Durang

Eurypides

Lorraine Hansberry

Lillian Hellman

Langston Hughes

William Inge

Lisa Kron

Tony Kushner

David Mamet

Terrance McNally

Arthur Miller

Moliere

Eugene O'Neill

Lori-Suzan Park

Harold Pinter

Theresa Rebeck

William Shakespeare

Sam Shepard

Neil Simon

Aaron Sorkin

Wendy Wasserstein

Oscar Wilde

Tennessee Williams

August Wilson

Some Films to View:

An Affair to Remember

All About Eve

Amadeus

The Apartment

Butch Cassidy and the Sundance Kid

Casablanca

Citizen Kane

A Clockwork Orange

The Deer Hunter

From Here to Eternity

The Godfather

The Godfather Part II

The Graduate

Ladybird

Mr. Smith Goes to Washington

On the Waterfront

One Flew Over the Cuckoo's Nest

Singin' in the Rain

Some Like It Hot

Taxi Driver

To Kill A Mockingbird

And when you're done with those—start making your way down the American Film Institute's greatest films of all-time list.

Some Television to Watch:

30 Rock

All in the Family

Arrested Development

Flea Bag

Freaks and Geeks

I Love Lucy

Mad Men

Roots (min-series)

Saturday Night Live (first few seasons to begin with)

Six Feet Under

Star Trek

The Handmaids Tale

The Mary Tyler Moore Show

The Sopranos
The West Wing

Some Actors: Study Their Work Across All Mediums:

Mahershala Ali

Javier Bardem

Angela Bassett

Cate Blanchett

Marlon Brando

Timothee Chalamet

Don Cheadle

Glenn Close

Tony Curtis

Bette Davis

Viola Davis

James Dean

Judi Dench

Mos Def

Benecio Del Toro

Robert DeNiro

Edie Falco

Judy Garland

Rachel Griffiths

Selma Hayek

Audrey Hepburn

Nicole Kidman

Jessica Lange

John Leguizamo

Daniel Day Lewis

Frances McDormand

Marilyn Monroe

Elisabeth Moss

Lupita Nyong'o

Laurence Olivier

Dev Patel

Sidney Poitier

Roger Rees

Alan Rickman

Saoirse Ronan

Mark Rylance

Marian Seldes

Octavia Spencer

Meryl Streep

John Voigt

Denzel Washington

Michelle Williams

Robin Williams

BD Wong

Alfre Woodard

Curiosity and the pursuit of knowledge of things foreign to you will be so valuable to you as an actor. You'll access emotions you never knew existed and be able to bring that much more to your work. Persist in learning!

Part 3
The Casting Director's Role on the Creative Team

12 What, Exactly, Does a Casting Director Do?

You might be surprised to learn that the job of a theatrical casting director is not very different from the job of an actor. The truth is that the type of groundwork that gets us to our side of the table requires the same kind of hard work that gets the actor into the audition room.

At the time of this writing, I am working with Tara Rubin, who is an institution in and of herself, so for the most part we get the job because of repeat business through hard-won and long-standing relationships with creative teams of writers, directors, music supervisors, choreographers and producers. Or the work may come via recommendations from other industry professionals. But in the beginning, before you've got a following and a proven track record, we pretty much do the same thing you do as actors to get a job.

Case in point:

ME: Hey, boss, I saw that John Doe is producing *blanket-y-blank* on Broadway next season. I really love this story and I really want to work with this director.

BOSS: Hmmmm—I don't know any of those guys. If you want it, go get it.
    Next day . . .

ME: On phone to every GM (general management company) in New York: "Hi, are you guys working on *Blanket-y-blank?*," till I find the right person. "Oh awesome! Is there a casting director attached yet? No?

Are you guys taking meetings? If so, I'd love to come in and meet on this project" (she said, heart pounding, hoping she doesn't get laughed at or hung up on).

Sound familiar?

If I'm lucky I get a positive response. Of course, it turns out that they are only meeting with people on the day I happen to be leaving for my first vacation in a year. But what's a two-hundred-dollar airline change fee if it means a chance at a job I really want?

Again, sound familiar?

Now begins the preparation. And the nerves. Yup—even now.

I do the work that sets me up to succeed—and it's not so different from the things you should be doing to get work as actors. I read up on everything I can about anyone involved—writers, composers, directors, actors these people have worked with and liked (or didn't) in the past.

I make lists of names of actors I envision in the leads, I jot down thoughts, I put packages together with pictures and resumes. I troll the internet cutting and pasting clips of performances that might help educate the creative team about certain performers. *I have no idea if I will even get to open up my binder or laptop at this meeting.* You know, like how sometimes you work on thirty pages of sides and music for an audition and you don't get asked for any of it? Yeah. Like that.

There have been many times where I was completely wrong about what I thought were inspired choices of what to say to the creative teams and how and when to say them and I walked out of my interview thinking I'd blown it and that I'd never see those people again.

But maybe the call comes that I do get the job. An official offer is made. There is very little negotiating. It's a sort of a take-it-or-leave-it offer. Everyone is apparently in "dire straits and agreeing to cut their fees."Oh. Ummm. Okay. Yes, absolutely, thank you!

So, I set about getting everyone's names, titles and contact info. I map out a potential audition schedule—which works for absolutely no one. The communiques about auditions go on for what feels like years.

Then I reserve studios (please God let there be something with natural light, big enough to dance in, open past 6:00 p.m., where the air conditioning doesn't hum and we can't hear the tappers in the room above). I hire audition accompanists and readers (actors who serve as scene partners for the auditioners). Then I mock-up audition notices for approval by producers. Then I post said notices. I sit for a solid week at the required round of union auditions. These auditions can be done in person or via self-tape, I field calls from agents. I pre-screen people. I callback people to audition for the associate creative team. I get wet paper towels for the dancers to step on so they don't slip while dancing and I make coffee runs and find space heaters for freezing studios or fans for sweltering ones. I do all this while never letting go of a suitcase filled with notes, sides, session sheets, sheet music, drum sticks, knee pads, bottled water, sign-in sheets and video equipment—whatever the day may require. You're seeing the parallels here, right?

Not only do casting directors and their associates and assistants set your audition appointments, send you audition materials, prepare you for your work sessions and callbacks, give you notes, secure the audition venues, accompanists and readers, but they also stand beside you, with you, and for you throughout your audition process. They are your cheerleaders and champions.

They are valued as and by industry creatives and executives for their knowledge of the actors' bodies of work—and *no less significantly*—for their knowledge of the actor as an individual: your temperament, your work ethic, your *reputation*. Casting directors are judged based on their ability to identify talent and the success, or not, of their opinions and suggestions. Their choices are scrutinized in much the same way your acting choices are scrutinized during the audition process.

Casting directors are not the enemy of the actor. We keep saying this but there seems to be a host of never-ending stories to the contrary. Some of those are true. Most are not and one bad apple doesn't spoil the whole bunch. We may be the only people who are actually aware of all that you're being asked to do to prepare for these auditions: the time and money and effort that goes into getting ready (hair, outfits, makeup, vocal coaching, self-taping, lighting) and we want to help you shine in your audition. When you're prepared, you make us look good. More importantly, when you're prepared, it frees you up to take a note, to truly be able to listen and stay in the moment, and that will speak not only to your talent but also to your work ethic—which *will* matter to the creative team.

You cannot throw a rock without hitting a casting director who was once an actor. So, give us the benefit of the doubt and remember we want you to be great.

As an actor I spent years auditioning for casting directors who were mostly total strangers. I had no idea who they were, much less what, besides calling me in for the audition, they, as casting directors, did. The one thing I did know, which caused a lot of anxiety, was that they were about to have a hand in determining my future. I came to realize that had I done my homework on the casting director and the rest of the creative team before walking into those audition rooms, at least some of my anxiety and fears would have been eliminated. When you audition, you should have at least some knowledge of the bodies of work of the casting directors and maybe even know a bit about their professional journeys.

You're living in an era where all kinds of information, not just professional, but personal, can be found in an instant on the internet. Had I been able to see on social media that, for instance, the director has a new baby, or that the choreographer just got married, that information would have helped humanize those people whose approval and respect I hoped to garner. That accessibility might have made me see them as more friends than foes. Seeing the creative team in that light might have helped me to believe that I was in that room because they truly were rooting for me. Do *your research* each and every time you audition *on everyone* you have reason to believe will be in the room.

Casting directors are integral members of the creative team who perform many variations of essentially the same job depending on which segment of the industry—live theater, television, or film—they work in. When it comes to studio and network casting for television and film there are a variety of more specific job titles than there are in legit (live) theater, but the hierarchies throughout the industry are basically the same: casting directors, associate casting directors, assistant to casting directors, interns.

Here is a general synopsis of what the various types of casting directors across the industry do:

Theater

Theater casting directors create and distribute the audition notices and breakdowns (a description of the casting requirements for a play or musical). They pre-screen (the very first audition in what can be a very long series of auditions) actors and callback the candidates that meet the needs of the project to audition for the associate creative team. Then together, they all decide who moves forward to the next phase of the casting process with the full creative team. If you make it to the final callbacks for a Broadway show, there will be dozens of decision-makers in the room. Among them will be the casting director, all the members of the creative team, their associates, and any number of producers and assorted assistants. The casting directors are often the conduit between the actor/agent/manager and the person representing the project (general managers—the GM's) who will actually make you an offer on behalf of the creative team. For the most part, once the contracts are negotiated and signed, the casting director is pretty much done until the show opens. Hopefully the show has enough success that they will be busy casting replacement actors for a very long time.

Television and Film

In film and television there are a wide variety of CDs, all with different responsibilities, although it is as a group that the best person for the role is decided upon. In this world, casting directors are hired after being approved by the studio making the television show or movie. Usually, casting directors get the job because a director or producer has asked for them specifically or they've competed for and booked the job, just as you do as an actor.

As a *studio* (television or production) *casting director*, the job is to:

- thoroughly know the needs of any given project
- identify actors who speak to the needs of the writing and producing team.

These *casting directors* oversee the independent casting folks the studio has hired to ensure that they are bringing in people the project creatives have described they want—speaking to concept, style, type, budget, and so on.

As a *television network casting executive* and as a *production (this can be television or film) studio casting executive*, the job is to:

- thoroughly know the needs of any given project
- to ensure that the needs (demographics, budget, contract terms, distribution, etc.) of the network are met.

These *casting executives* truly need to be visionaries so that everyone (corporate *and* creative) gets what they need and want (or the best balance of the two as a compromise) in the end.

All these types of casting directors serve different masters and as a result, have varying reasons for accepting or rejecting actors for a job. It's a miracle when an actor ticks every box for all the casting directors and executives involved in a film or television project. There are just an infinite number of variables involved in every casting process.

And sometimes, no matter how hard you try, you're just not going to be able to know all about every single nuance of a project or all about every single decision maker in the room. But *knowledge is power* so just do your best to be as informed as possible.

13 The Casting Director and the Audition Process

Your first point of contact in an audition for professional theater, film, and television will be the casting director. They are the people who are there at the very beginning—the ones responsible for actually putting the talent in the room at the very start of a project. Once you've been selected by the casting director to move forward in the audition process, you will then be seen by the rest of the creative team. The casting director will be with you as you work your way through the many steps of the audition process. You'll be glad to have them along for that roller coaster ride because the casting process can be long and arduous and they're your staunchest supporters. You can be secure in the knowledge that the casting director is doing everything in their power to help you succeed.

In a perfect world, you'll be getting lots of callbacks and booking lots of jobs. And in a perfect world, the sequence of events throughout the audition process would be linear and make sense. However, casting is a creative endeavor and as such is conducted on constantly shifting ground. Since the goal of this book is to demystify the casting process, I'll outline the series of auditions the actor goes through. But *caveat*—it is subject to change.

Theater

Theater casting directors put out the breakdowns for the productions. The breakdown contains information on character descriptions, contract type, a summary of the piece, and lists of the creative team (director, writers, etc.) members. The breakdown is electronically sent to a company called Breakdown Services to be posted on their website. Your agent or manager, who hopefully has an account with that service, will log on every day, look at what's auditioning and submit you via the website. Casting directors log on to the site to view the agent submissions for all of their projects and decide who they want to see.

Now a notice gets emailed to Actors Equity Union when/if an Equity call (audition) is required by the union. Because there are different rules for different types of contracts within the Actors Equity union, an Equity call may or may not be required. The notice states where and when the required calls will take place and what kind of materials the actor should prepare. Equity actors can log in daily to the Equity website to view the information and decide which auditions to go to. These notices are also posted in trade papers and on other websites, Actors Access and Playbill.com, for example, so that non-union actors also have the means to know about Equity calls and attend in the hopes there may be time for non-union actors to be seen.

Depending on the casting needs, ads might also be placed in trade papers or on social media to let people know about open-call auditions. Open calls (which are open to everyone) are not the same as union-required Equity calls and are done at the discretion of the creative teams. Any actor can attend these open calls—even if they're not a union member. These usually happen in the city of origin (city where the whole audition process is happening) and/or where the show is actually happening. Casting directors will also travel to different cities to hold open calls.

In a perfect world, the audition process for legit theater would happen in the following order—but it bears repeating—this is often subject to change—usually based on team and actor availability. (I've included steps for musical auditions here. Obviously for plays those steps don't apply.)

- Open calls (again, union and non-Union actors may attend these) and the required Actors Equity union calls. This initial round of auditions is usually conducted by the lead casting director on the project. Hopefully the candidates will move on to the next phase. Usually, actors perform their own material for these initial auditions.

- Callback auditions with the lead casting director. The actor will have an appointment for this audition. At this time, the casting director will also audition actors who perhaps didn't attend the first round of auditions, but whose work is known by the casting office. This is when the actor will receive show materials to learn for their audition. The successful candidates from this round will move on to the next step.

- Once the casting director has selected a pool of potential talent whom they believe meet the needs of the production, the actors are called in to be seen by the associate creative team members to read (and sing where applicable). Once that round is finished, it is decided who moves forward to the next phase of the casting process.

- Callback auditions with the associate creative team. For this round of auditions, the actors are seen a second time by the associate creative team—the associate director, the music department, and the dance department are added around this stage, as this is usually the point where the dance auditions begin.

- Dance callbacks (if it's a musical) are scheduled to further explore the skills of the potential company members.

Candidates will be auditioned again to further identify and consider strengths in style and skill (jazz, tap, hip hop, partnering abilities, etc.). You'll need appropriate shoes and, in some situations, knee pads. It's your responsibility to be prepared and to bring whatever is required.

- Work sessions are scheduled for potential candidates when the associate creative team wants more information on the skills and to further evaluate the potential of the actors. The actor might be asked to work with any member of the creative team (which you'll notice has grown exponentially since the first audition!) to explore whether or not their skill set best matches those required by the piece. It is the work session for some actors that determine whether they are then cut or will move on to the final callbacks.

- Final callbacks. If you make it to the final callbacks there will be dozens of decision-makers in the room. Among them will be the casting directors, all the members of the creative team, their associates, and any number of producers. Your final audition might also be videotaped and sent to any decision maker who was unable to be present.

Once this series of auditions has been completed, a whole new phase of evaluations begins. All of those candidates still in the mix are considered on the basis of yet another set of needs— the way actors look together and their potential chemistry. If it is a musical, this is when we can start to think about the tone and voice quality and whether or not the voices of the actors who are still "in the mix" will blend. The creatives will go through a process of collaborating on how to best arrange the actors and their roles according to the needs of the production. For every actor cast in the role, another actor, or two, is needed to understudy that role. Sometimes rather than an understudy, the size of the role requires a stand-by (someone whose only job is to be ready to go on at a moment's notice for one specific role. They are not otherwise on stage every night in the way ensemble members who understudy leads are). And of course, due to budget constraints, the size of the cast is finite. So, the creative team is tasked with figuring out the best combination of actors who can best populate the most efficient combination of roles/understudies. And they need to identify a few people who are capable of, let's say, understudying all of the women in the ensemble or perhaps two or three very different types of principal roles. Or any number of combinations thereof.

Once the structure of the roles and the formula for which actors assigned to which parts will understudy which other roles (a challenging puzzle for everyone involved) is set, the final cast is decided on, and offers are made.

At this point, the casting director acts as the conduit between the actor's agent and/or manager, or the actor themselves, and the general manager of the project who will actually be the one who makes the offer on behalf of the project and the creative team.

Sometimes, during the deal-making process the casting directors are brought into the conversation by the general managers to help move the deal-making process along. Some of the questions they might be called upon to answer are—"Is this guy really worth what he's asking?," "Do you have back-ups if we can't make a deal with this actor?" And the casting director will know enough about the actors to offer up solutions like—"This actor has a family—if you can't go higher on salary, offer two roundtrip tickets during the course of the contract so the kids can visit, that might do it." Or, "Let him bring his dog," "... have a car to himself," or "Offer to travel her bike on the tour truck." Hopefully negotiations are successful and the actor will accept the job.

But sometimes, the actor who is the first choice for the role will turn it down or become unavailable. When that happens, the actor who is in the backup position (provided we've even got a backup) moves ahead and *that* can cause a domino effect resulting in a complete reassignment of roles. So it goes, role by role, actor by actor, until a full company is finally cast.

Television and Film

In television and film, it's more difficult to learn about the majority of audition opportunities if you don't have an agent or a manager. But as always, the internet is your friend. Be diligent about checking for auditions on websites such as Backstage.com, Playbill.com and the like.

The casting department at the television or film production studio—say Touchstone or Dreamworks or Warner Brothers or Nickelodeon—has a whole department of casting people and they each have a title within their own hierarchy. The purpose of the studio casting *director* is to speak to the needs of the creative team which is composed of the writers and producers. As a studio casting *executive*, the job is to oversee the independent casting folks (the ones who actually bring in the talent) and see to it that they are bringing in people the creatives have described they want—speaking to concept, style, type, affordability, and so on.

Your first point of contact will be the independent casting director. And, once you have your appointment for an audition in television—for simplicity, we'll say this is an audition for a series regular—the progression of steps will be, generally, the following:

Television

- The independent casting director, who is hired by the television production studio, will conduct pre-screen auditions. The actor will be given sides (cuts from the script) or a few pages of script to work with. If you succeed on this level, you'll move to the next step.

- Callbacks with the project's producers are next. If you're an actor whose work is known to those in charge of the project, the pre-screen will be skipped and this will be your first step in the audition process. If successful at this level, you'll move forward.

- Work sessions with the producers and writers—who are frequently one and the same—will follow.

- Those who are still in the mix will do a "test" with executives at the production studio. This is the final callback to be sure that all the needs of the creative team are being met. Should you be successful at this level, you will be moved along to do a "test" for the casting executives at the network level.

- The network test will follow, with the same people as before in the room, plus *all* of the network executives. And by *all*, I mean as many as twenty to twenty-five decision-makers. Among them may be executive producers (I have seen up to ten of these on one project alone), director, consulting producers, showrunners, writers, business affairs lawyers, network presidents, programming executives, development executives, senior vice presidents of casting from the network and the studio, vice presidents of casting from the network and studio and lots and lots of assistants.

The network casting executives have a hierarchy of their own— director of casting, that person's assistant, vice president of casting and their staff, senior vice president of casting and their staff, and so on. The network executive is not only in on the ultimate approval of the actors but also has day-to-day tasks that are a little different than those of the studio casting executive.

Casting executives at a television network are charged with knowing the network's specific demographic. So on any given day it's their job to go to the creators of a project and say something like, "I see why you like that actor but one of the reasons we are spending a billion dollars to make your pilot is because, based on knowing our demographic needs, you pitched that role as relatable to men in the Bible Belt between the ages of 30 and 55. We are lacking viewership there and this actor **doesn't** speak to that type-wise and we need one who **does**." Or, "The network wants to build their teenage audience—this actor won't appeal to that demographic." And now after all your hard work and a series of excellent auditions, you're out of the running. But that's the business of the *business*. The sooner you accept that reality, the better off you will be.

If you're being called in for any other roles (guest star, co-star, etc.) it will be an abbreviated process and may even simply involve approval via video audition, in which case the independent casting director simply puts actors on tape and sends them along to the production studio casting folks. For guest and co-star roles it is much more possible to be made an offer strictly on the merits of your video and you may never even have to audition in person. This casting is usually fast and furious depending on when/if that week's episode's script is available.

The network casting executives are the ones who work with the business affairs department (the network's lawyers) to make offers and close deals. While streaming and other internet platform series contracts are constantly evolving, often as a regular on a network television series, an actor is signed for as many as seven years. And here's a fun fact—for a series regular or sometimes even a recurring role (recurring roles will have a story arc and the actor may be asked to sign on for three-to-six episodes only)—the actor who is testing at the network level must have a closed deal *before* they are allowed to audition. Yep. No one wants to negotiate with you once you know we want you. So, and this is huge—you, the actor, basically sign away a substantial chunk of your life before you've even got the job.

Often these negotiations are still going on while you're in the waiting room on the very day of your audition. The business affairs lawyers are feverishly trying to close the deal with your agents. Three hours later you still haven't gone in and now you're a mess. The casting director for the network does their best to try and help keep the deal moving along so that you can get in there and do your best work.

In television, the director is not always involved in casting because once the show is successful and well established each episode of a series often has a different director. However, on the day of the first table read (the first day the whole company gathers around a table to read through the script), should the director not be happy with an actor hired (usually to be a guest or co-star), they may ask to have that actor replaced. Yet another hurdle for the actor—many have been replaced after the table read. That said, there are no set rules and sometimes the director *is* involved in the TV audition process right from the start.

Film

The casting process for film is much the same, if a bit abbreviated, as it is for television.

- Pre-screen auditions with the independent casting director.
- Callbacks with the project's writers and producers. Once again, if you're an actor whose work is known to those in charge of the project, the pre-screen will be skipped and this will be your first step in the audition process. Once successful at this level, you'll move forward.

- The remaining candidates are put on film or tested, aka screen tested, for the director and movie studio executives for final approval.

A screen test is usually a pretty big deal in that it takes so many people to make it happen. Suddenly you are on a campus of a production or movie company. Sometimes you'll be in someone's empty office and there'll be one camera, the camera operator, the person reading the scene with you and a handful of the creative team, including, this time, the director of the pilot or the film. But more often than not, you'll be ushered onto a soundstage or into a studio where you will get your hair and makeup done—at the very least, touched up—and you'll walk to the shooting area and there will be A LOT of people milling about: the sound and lighting people, Casting, and any number of studio and/or network executives. You'll then read your scenes as you did in the rooms at the beginning of the process. You'll hear, "Action!" You'll hear, "CUT!" and it will all be for YOU. It's exciting and fun and nerve-racking and you'll allow yourself to imagine if you got to do this all the time. AND get paid for it. AND be famous! The purpose of a screen test is varied but it most often happens when the creatives and executives feel they need to see you on screen—feel how you come across in a medium that is very different from seeing someone live. Sometimes this also serves as a chance for what we call a "chemistry read" with an actor you will potentially be playing opposite. If you're testing, you can be pretty sure that this is the final audition and that after the test, a decision will be made.

The fact of the matter is that the only guarantee is that the path you travel in the casting process will be different every single time you audition. Just keep a positive attitude as you move forward and remember you're there because the casting director thinks you're right for the role and wants you to succeed.

Part 4
Auditions

14 Auditions

On Being Prepared

We casting directors always do our best to prepare you for the unexpected but you never know what will be asked of you and oftentimes we don't either. Make sure you do everything you possibly can within your range of knowledge to be ready for a curveball.

For example, I spent one long afternoon and evening frantically calling the agents of every actor in the final mix of *Young Frankenstein* because EGOT (Emmy, Grammy, Oscar, and Tony Award) winner Mel Brooks called our office the day before the final callbacks—he wrote the book of this musical as well as the film—and requested that the actors be completely off book so that he could get up and work with them script free. If you're Mel Brooks, that's a perfectly reasonable request, but for you, the actor who is about to have a master class with one of the greatest comedic geniuses of all time, it's quite the last-minute "ask" prep-wise.

Another memorable case in point—on the day of the invited dance call for the Broadway revival of *Promises, Promises* I had been running ragged fetching water and coffee and trying to make everyone comfortable. It had been pouring rain all day and we had a holding room filled with soggy, sweaty dancers waiting to come in to audition in groups. They would do a combination for the choreographer and other creative team members, and then some of the dancers would be cut and then some others would be called in to learn another combination. The audition room was a huge windowless studio with mirrors covering one long wall and a lot of folding chairs set up along the mirror facing the dancers, with a piano off to the side. Perfect—but it had lousy cell and internet service. I had been running outside to check my messages and emails from time to time. Amid all the running in and out, I saw Mr. Neil Simon, who wrote the book for the show and who is one of the most revered playwrights of all time, arrive to watch the dance auditions. Neil Simon at a dance call? No one knew he was coming. There's no way to prepare for that, except to breathe, smile and try to stay focused.

I have a *lot* to say about my idea of what it truly means to be prepared for an audition versus what the actor thinks it means to be prepared for an audition. Most actors don't even know what information to gather, what questions to ask, or why knowing the answers might actually give them a leg up!

Of course, you are going to be as familiar as possible with the material. Of course, you will have made strong, vivid acting choices. Of course, the character you create will have a point of view. In addition to all that, when you walk into an audition room, you'll be better prepared if you know—at the very least—the following:

- Who's in the room?
- The prior works of the creative team members
- Who have they cast in other shows?
- If you have mutual friends with any of the creatives

Actors who know *the room* are likely to book more than the ones who don't. The more you know about the people in the room, the more comfortable you'll feel. Knowledge is power.

Walking In

Actors are always asking how they should walk into the audition room and what the casting directors look for when an actor first walks through the door. Well, how do you walk into an interview? *Any* interview? Why is it that so many actors do not take the same tack when they enter the audition room?

I had a young actor audition for a musical—for the role of a man who is mostly quiet throughout the play until he is moved to violence. He was asked to come in and read and sing and was told he may be asked to stay for a dance call later that afternoon. He literally leaped into the room and took a big bow while introducing himself. You guys get that that kind of entrance can't be un-seen, right? Do yourselves a favor and think this stuff through. Nerves contribute to so much of what happens in the audition room. Don't make the mistake of not giving the nerves the credence they deserve. How do you act and react when you are nervous? Do you make jokes? Talk a lot? Find it hard to catch your breath? Do your nerves somehow manifest themselves physically—like with our friend the "leaper"? An audition is a professional interview. Act accordingly.

Walking in is just that—an entrance. You've been invited into the room, now it's time for you to demonstrate that you belong there. Simply hold your head high and conduct yourself with the confidence and grace that comes with being absolutely prepared. Then smile, say hello, and get to work.

I've heard plenty of people say that casting directors and creatives make decisions about you within the first ten seconds you're in the room. In my experience this is just not true. But if nothing I say will persuade you otherwise, then just be sure to walk into the room with the most polished professional presence you can muster.

What you *leave us with* as an actor is what ultimately counts. How you've dealt with your reader or accompanist, how well you know your material, the choices you've made as actors, how you take and execute adjustments you're given—those are the things we're watching. So, please let go of the concept that a final decision about whether or not you're right for the role will be made within the first few seconds of walking into the room.

And please know that sometimes the vibes in these rooms are not warm and fuzzy. We're working. Don't let the mood of the room spook you. It was that way before you arrived and has absolutely nothing to do with you, so stay your course.

Bring Your Tools

Your tools are your armory of audition materials—your sides, your songs, monologues, pictures, resumes, clothes, your *attitude*.

When you do have the luxury of choosing your own audition materials, make your choices based on the stories you are passionate about telling. Whether it's an audition for film, television or theater, we know it is impossible to show us your entire bag of tricks in only one audition. All we need from any first audition is a glimmer—something that makes us want to explore you further.

Your *choices* are also your tools. I know for a fact that some actors—consciously or not—decide to try and show that they do a lot of things kind of well. I think it's because on some level they're worried that if they are *too* specific, casting directors will only see you as *that*. Forever. But if you've made a bold, original, truthful choice—not one that simply makes you think you'll stand out or that is somehow gimmicky, even if that bold, original, truthful choice doesn't work, I'll still think—well that's not right for *this*, but she's interesting, and *that* was a smart choice. I wonder what else she can do? You will never be punished for being too specific.

Acting requires technique, knowledge, and immersion in many genres and styles, so it's impossible to have material perfectly suited for every one of them. But just to be safe, here's what I recommend to have at the ready at all times:

For Theater, Television, and Film: Monologues—(Age Appropriate!)

- One serious CLASSICAL
- One comedic CLASSICAL
- One serious MODERN
- One comedic MODERN

And please—I shouldn't have to say this but apparently, *I do*: If you're auditioning for a previously published play, please have read the *entire* play and know who wrote it so that you can speak on it intelligently if asked.

For Musical Theater, Television, and Film: Audition Songs

- One pop ballad
- One true rock and roll hardcore, edgy ballad
- One up-tempo pop and/or rock song
- One traditional musical theater ballad
- One traditional up-tempo musical theater song.

Have solid sixteen-bar cuts of each song, but *also be prepared to sing that entire song if asked to do so*. When you are asked for sixteen bars, choose wisely. Your choices should always be about acting first and foremost. You'll want cuts with story arcs. Most songs are structured so that they can be cut into sixteen or thirty-two bar cuts. Find songs and experiment with how to cut them using those amounts of measures (give or take) that can tell a full story. Wherever you start your cut, that should be the beginning of your story, your "once upon a time."

Eventually, as you grow your song book, you'll add specialty songs—little ditties that don't have to reinvent the wheel but will be perfect for showing your emotional range or your special brand of quirkiness and comedic skills.

I'm frequently asked if it is better to show your vocal or your emotional range. Ummmmm, yes! Whenever possible, try to show both in one song. When that's not possible, always choose the song that best reflects the world of the piece for which you're auditioning.

Just to be clear, by vocal range, we mean how high or low you sing. By emotional range we mean how capable you are of intimating the world you're auditioning for. We are interested in *your* interpretations of that—not in how you've seen it done before.

What's impressive to us is when an actor chooses a piece because *they* are challenged by it—because it asks that they stretch *themselves*. And if you do choose the songs that are universally known to be difficult or are particularly identified with a certain artist—*do not take the responsibility lightly*. You will be judged based on your merit but also on our expectations because we've heard versions of it that are iconic.

Music Should Suit Your Sound

Your song should suit your sound. Maybe you've been asked for a pop/rock song. While you'll want to capture the style of the show for which you're auditioning as best you can with the knowledge you have, remember Billy Joel and The Rolling Stones are both in the rock and roll vein but have very different sounds. Choose the style that you think fits *your* sound best.

To Transpose or Not to Transpose?

As I've said before, the reason you should choose a piece is because you are passionate about the story. You may be in love with the song, but if you have to change the key, it may not be the best choice for you and may not show you in your best light.

Think long and hard about changing the key. Composers write in a certain key because they want the sound of your voice to match the emotion they envision. You don't want to mess with songs that have built-in expectations. *Defying Gravity* for example—the expectation is that you'll be able to kill songs of this ilk in their original keys. If an iconic song is in a bad key for you—*choose something else*. The key is part of what makes it iconic.

The flipside is that with many songs, because the key is not essential to the emotion involved in the storytelling, the key makes absolutely no difference, so there's no reason not to have it transposed. All due respect to the composer, *for your purposes*, the key is negligible. You'll just have to use your own judgment.

If you're passionate about a song that's not written in your key, find the key that is most comfortable for you and have it transposed. That way, you have a chart that is all yours—a song you've really made your own—it might even turn into your signature piece. That is an instance where your money would be well spent. If you're asked why you transposed the song in an audition, answer truthfully, for example, this is a story I'm passionate about telling and feel the song itself, my version of it, is appropriate for this audition. You should be able to offer other song options. Know that they may ask you to vocalize if they are concerned about your vocal range.

You might want to turn a serious song into a funny one or vice-versa. Everyone behind the table will have a different opinion on this. It's risky. If you choose to do it, commit to doing it fully and professionally.

Do *not* sing a song that is *at all uncomfortable for you vocally*— not on a "good" day, a "bad" day (you have a cold or you're losing your voice) or any other day! It's possible that in the long run, you'll do serious vocal damage.

Communicate with Your Accompanist

Your music needs to be in a three-ring binder. Make sure it is printed double-sided. The pages should not be encased in glare-inducing plastic and they should be easy to turn. Don't expect your accompanist to be a mind reader—your music should be clearly marked.

This is how the conversation with the accompanist should go:

Hi, this is where I start, this is where I end. Please don't take the repeat. This is my tempo (demonstrate tempo by tapping your chest, or by quietly singing a little bit of the piece). There may be further instructions. For example, in this section I speak, or, please play this section softly, as if underscoring. But you want to keep your instructions as simple as possible. If it takes much longer than a minute to communicate your needs to the accompanist, it's too complicated. Keep it simple *or* bring your own accompanist. Make sure your music is marked as you'd like it played. Your accompanist may not remember all your instructions, but if your music is correctly and legibly marked, there shouldn't be a problem.

Overcoming Nerves

No matter how many auditions you've survived, you're still going to have to contend with nerves and all the problems they bring. For example—in a musical theater audition, if you know you are not a chronically pitchy singer but you're having some issues because of nerves (when you're nervous the first thing to go is your breath and without breath control you might have pitch issues to contend with) you should *stop*. *Start again*. Maybe you need to communicate with your accompanist—check a note or change the tempo. Take a breath. Remind yourself to keep breathing. Whatever you do—*fix it if you can*—*quickly and efficiently*. We'll respect that. It is acceptable to do so as long as you're not already halfway done with your song.

In any situation, film, television or theater, take control of your own audition. If you feel yourself getting flustered and going downhill and don't put on the brakes, you've got no one to blame but yourself for a bad outcome. It's good when we know that you *recognize* that you are having an issue and are capable of making it right.

Getting Ready to Go In and Sing

Make sure your audition is the second time you sing your audition piece that day. Sing at the top of your lungs as you walk down the street or rent a studio for fifteen minutes and sing through everything before you go in. Now that you've done that, you know you've got at least one in you today, but maybe not two—better to know that in advance so that you can decide if you need to make a different choice later on in the audition. You can sing through it six hours before the audition or six minutes before. This is not about the warming up your voice part. This is about the getting one under your belt part. The second time is always better, so let your audition be the second time. Don't forget to do your sides full-out, too—it's equally important to have the rhythm and pacing of the text be effortless in the moment. Know where you're going to turn the page and what comes at the top of the next page.

If you're singing something on a day when you feel like maybe you've only got one in you, unless you've been given material from the show to learn, *choose something easier.* You don't know what will be asked of you in there. You must feel confident about your stamina and protect your vocal health.

You should be approaching your songs just like you would your monologue or sides. Find the beats; the emotional turns. Play with phrasing—everything doesn't have to be sung the way you heard it on the cast album. Speak the song aloud, not in the rhythm of the song, but as you would in a normal conversation. Take note of what you are *naturally* emphasizing. This will help inform your acting choices. You must start and finish strong. While we may forget what happens in the middle ("may" being the operative word), we *will* remember your beginning and your ending.

Take a moment before you start singing to remember why it's so important for you to tell this story. Think about what happened in the storyline, be it the one in the piece or one of your own imaginings, of the song right before you start singing. Think about what made you have to tell this story. Maybe your song is a reaction or an answer to a question you've been asked. Think about what the character wants to accomplish before the song is over. What are the stakes? Do you want to keep someone from leaving? Do you want someone to know you love them? Are you looking for safety? Comfort? Work and rework these songs until you cannot think of one thing you haven't yet tried.

And, this is *important*—adjust your performance for the audition room. You are not yet in full costume standing on the lip of the stage with a spotlight on your face. We are two feet from you. We can see the raise of an eyebrow. Just because you are completely natural doesn't mean we will worry that you can't project or that your performance won't fill a 2,000-seat house. *Keep it real.*

What to Wear

While you certainly don't need to wear exactly what you are wearing in your photos—it bears repeating that the person walking in the door should look like the person in the photo. Furthermore, the clothes you choose should at least suggest your idea of the world of the piece for which you're auditioning.

For Film and Television

If you're auditioning for the role of an assistant district attorney on a TV drama, you'll want to wear business attire. Even though you might also have a scene that shows you in a casual environment, it's a court room TV drama and that's the predominant image we need to have stick with us. Just "suggest" with your clothes and be comfortable in them.

For Theater

No more the jewel-toned dresses and character heels of yesteryear as a uniform for everything. I do not mean you need to don an apron and carry a tray if you are reading for the role of a waiter—it'd be totally cheesy to be too literal. But do think about a person whose world is a busy, upscale restaurant— maybe try comfortable shoes and black pants and a white shirt.

If you're a male auditioning for *Jersey Boys* and you come in wearing cargo shorts and flip-flops—how does this help you? The play takes place in an era when people were more formal— these guys were sharp. They wore sports coats and dress shoes. People ironed their clothes.

You hold yourself differently when wearing tailored pants and dress shoes than you do in jeans and sneakers. Control the things you can control. Set yourself up for success wherever you can. I believe this also shows a level of care. Go that extra mile.

Now the *caveat*—you must feel comfortable and confident in whatever you choose to wear. Be wary of new shoes that might start to hurt before you've even gotten off the subway or borrowing stuff from friends that don't really fit you. That discomfort will be stressful and that will show in your body language.

I know it sounds like I'm making too big a deal about this, but if you are not comfortable in your own skin when you walk into a room, about to show us who you are, then that's just one more thing to worry about. And it's an unnecessary one. You've got enough on your plate. Feel great in what you're wearing.

Video Auditions

There will be times when you can get cast without having auditioned in person–especially in television. We have a lot of occasions where we will need to send a link of your work to the creative team. At the very least, self-taping is often the start of the audition process.

I send materials for actors to self-tape all the time. Maybe you're out of town and I want to see you on tape to determine whether it's worth it to ask you to fly in for an audition. Or, maybe there's no budget for in-person auditions because we are just in the developmental stage but the creatives still need to be educated on who you are.

No fancy or expensive equipment is necessary. Although you might find that purchasing a plain backdrop, of a color that suits you on camera and a good mic will make you feel more confident about the end product. Just be sure to show a full body shot at the beginning, remember to slate (state your name, your height, where you're based, and if you can be "local hire"—which means you won't expect to be compensated for relocating) and then you can zoom in at your discretion for the rest of the video. Always be sure that the sound is clear and the lighting is good. It's a good idea to send the video to yourself first so that you can address any technical difficulties others may encounter when opening the file.

There are videographers who specialize in audition taping, so if you'd feel better having someone else deal with the technical stuff, do that. If you're a novice at self-taping, it might be a good idea to see a professional when you're first starting out. They will even create the link for your clip. Just know it can get expensive and sometimes when last-minute auditions come up, that route may not be available to you.

For the most part, all you really need is a trusted camera phone, a blank wall and a well-lit room. If we can see you and hear you, that's all we require. Just send us something *clean* and we'll take it from there.

Taking Meetings—Another Type of Audition

In essence there are two types of meetings (also known as "generals"). Often agents and managers will be very keen for you to have a get-to-know-you meeting with casting directors or studio executives or with a director or music director—in short anyone who functions as a creative in the industry. It's a meet and greet of sorts, an introduction, in the hopes that now you will be at the forefront of that person's mind.

In theater it might go like this: an agent for a well-known television actor will contact me because they're a client who is interested in doing theater and is going to be in New York next week. The agent asks me, the casting director, to sit down with their client, the actor, and discuss potential projects that might be appropriate for them. This is just a few minutes during which, the agent hopes, results in that actor piquing my interest. I might not have thought of them as being interested in doing theater, but now I know, and will think of them going forward.

Here's another kind of meeting. The director of *The King and I* at Lyric Opera of Chicago wants to meet with superstar Jane Doe. But because Jane Doe feels her body of work should serve as her audition, Jane would expect to be offered a job outright. So, I'll ask her agent if she will just meet with that director. This gives them both the chance to sniff each other out, hear each other's thoughts on the project, and decide if they can get excited about spending a few months working together.

Very often when an actor is new to an agency or management company, the representative wants to introduce the client to the players in a given community—the casting executives at the networks, the producers of the hot Broadway show, the creatives at a popular streaming platform such as Netflix. That actor might be coached by their agent or manager on giving "good couch" (the art of being as charming and personable as the best guests on television talk show sofas). Depending on the project, the actor might be given some topics to bring up in the conversation during the meeting or some ideas on what the actor can bring up to show the most appealing part of their personality and in general how to leave these creatives with a positive impression and the desire to work with the actor. If no coaching beforehand happens, and you feel ill-prepared, seek advice from your agent or actor friends who have been down that road.

Sit down with your agent with a list of people you'd like to meet. Maybe you've never met the head of casting at a network. One new person in your corner can lead to a slew of auditions and can jumpstart your career. Be proactive when these opportunities arise. If you can get some meetings and leave a good impression, that can lead to a fresh round of auditions for industry folks that may not have seen you before. If you don't have an agent, then you have to figure out a way to meet these people on your own. This is just another aspect of networking.

Your Internet Presence—Yet Another Type of Audition

Many of us have a love-hate relationship with social media, but the fact is that you must have an internet presence. While its purpose is to connect us, like most good things, we've taken it to a level of distraction but I'm all for technology when it uses its powers for good.

There are many wonderful ways the internet will be your friend. Here's a "for instance" for you. Someone I know saw you at the New York City cabaret room *54 Below* last night. My friend knows I need a last-minute replacement for a benefit I'm casting and they think you might be perfect for that replacement. If you've posted a video on your website or on YouTube of your performance, I can find it and suggest you for the benefit. You step in and the music director of that benefit also happens to be the music director for an upcoming Lab (a workshop of sorts) of a new show that is slated for Broadway next year, and they ask you to be part of it because they were so impressed with your work at the benefit.

An instance where the internet is *not* your friend—casting directors may use social media as a platform to get the word out about an open call, but that does not mean you use that post to ask for an audition, or to "personal message" the casting director via social media. This is not an acceptable way to conduct business.

And, don't ever forget that what you post, no matter where you do so, is no longer just your own business. Assume that everyone is seeing everything and that they will form an opinion about you whether they've met you or not. Be mindful!

And, as long as we're talking about the internet, let's discuss what I like to call *insta-stars*. These are people who post their thoughts and particular skills, gather followers, and suddenly are considered professional actors. Okay—if they can sell tickets, if their followers are buying, they are now as viable as anyone.

In very few instances, these people find careers that last, but that's rare. More often than not, they go the way of most people who get their fifteen minutes of fame with no skills to back it up. Reality TV doesn't make actors. It makes people who get chances sometimes. So by all means, if your dream is to be a contestant on *The Amazing Race*, go for it. If you're talked about enough in the chat rooms, you may get an offer to play yourself as a guest star on a sitcom. But it is rare that you will be taken seriously or that you'll have any longevity unless you start developing some true acting technique. Those who *do* find a life as an actor after having won a huge singing contest (and these people at least come to us with natural born talent), are the people who know that *now* is when the real work begins— the classes, the coaching, the hard work of the craft—if they want to be competitive in this industry.

My advice is to do the work. Remember it's a marathon, not a sprint. That means that it is not enough to have a good audition or to be able to pull "tricks" out that make people like you. Eventually you will be revealed as a fake and it'll be over. Short cuts are just that—*short*. Like your careers may be. Do the work.

In other news regarding the internet, there is product *everywhere*. There are original movies and series, and all sorts of content being created by so many different platforms. Don't overlook opportunities in any market.

After the Audition

Ah the old feedback conundrum. When is it appropriate to ask for it and why?

Half the time I get emails from agents and actors asking for feedback before I've even left the audition room for the day. I understand the need for feedback, but you'll rarely get it. If you don't get a callback, chances are you're not going further with the project right at that moment, but that may or may not be true of the future.

When it is a pre-screen situation and only the casting person is in the room, then of course we know why we're not calling you back, but once the team is present, it's not my call anymore. The end of the day comes and we go down the session sheet and this is what we hear from the team: "yes, yes, no, yes, no, yes, no, no." I am not in a position to say to the director for each "no," "But why?"

Now I probably do know why, but do I want *you* to know "why"? Do I really want to be the one to tell you that someone in the room said that you were a pain in the neck during your last job? Do you need to know that when we called you in we didn't yet have our leading lady but now we do and you're too short for her? And if you just didn't sing well that day or take an adjustment quickly enough—well the truth is, you already know that, don't you? As a human being, I understand that some satisfaction is taken from knowing why it didn't happen for you that day, but there aren't enough hours in the day to get that info to every actor who wants it and doesn't mean that you're permanently off the radar for this show. Knowing all that stuff might help you improve. It just might also make you a nervous wreck.

If you're getting callbacks right and left and not booking anything and this goes on for a long while—then you might want to try and get some feedback and see if it is consistent— only then will you know if you need to make some changes. What would really be much more productive for you is to maybe make some adjustments in your general approach— warm up more thoroughly, make bolder choices, change up your audition material. Take your best guess at why what you're doing in the room isn't working, switch it up and see if it makes a difference.

I know how frustrating it is to hear our "stock" answers: "We just went a different way." "Just wasn't a good fit." "Nothing he could have done better or differently—it just didn't feel spot-on." There are a lot of puzzle pieces here and these answers are as true and specific as we are probably going to get. So just do your job. Audition. When you're not working as an actor, your job is to audition. And then do your best to let it go once you've left the room.

I speak only for myself here but unless I can give you something specific (the material is just too high for your vocal range, this character may wind up recurring on the series and you look too much like someone on the show) and productive and in a kind way, I'm not saying anything. What if I tell you the reason it's never going to happen and then the end of the audition process comes and something vital has changed and they want to go back to you? You might think you won't care because you're getting back in the room, but once you've heard something said it can't be taken back and it will affect you. It's just not possible to answer everyone's requests for notes, so if you don't get feedback, please don't take it personally.

15 The Self-Tape Audition

Here's the thing about self-tapes. The self-tape has become a way of life for the actor. Most actors can see the pros and cons of the self-tape but they are still divided and very conflicted about how they feel about them. One actor expressed their concern to me that, *"Self-taping is like acting in a void because of the lack of human contact."* Another said, *"There was a community and camaraderie that made the audition process bearable. Now that doesn't exist."* Yet another said, *"I couldn't seem to book a job in the room but the self-tape reduced my anxiety and I was able to do much better work."* Another said, *"self-tapes allow you to audition from out of town but it does take the human element out,"* and another worried, *"I don't even know if it was watched. At least in person you know you've been seen."*

The fear here is that the virtual world will somehow begin to dominate humanity and start wiggling its way into acting. Already special effects have changed how we feel when we watch a movie and even a live play. I know some will say that the objections to them usually come from the old school, more "mature" generations because it's new technology, but this is not a generational issue. It's an emotional one for the actor.

I wonder if when someone picks this book up in the not-too-distant future, whether this will still be an issue for actors. Perhaps some other technology may come along to replace this format. Or perhaps the industry may start to reject it. But right now, it's an industry standard that looks like it's here to stay.

The biggest reason self-taping is non-negotiable nowadays and isn't likely to change any time soon, is because technology has made it possible to find, explore, and consider actors for jobs who don't necessarily live where the auditions are taking place. I had a television director say to me, "*Tapes are essential. I can cast from my desk. Plus, the talent pool widens to the point it is global.*" And a film director told me—for better or worse, I can't decide—"*I can watch a hundred tapes in the time it takes to do a ten-person session and I don't have to worry about the actor's feelings.*" And to temper that harsh reality, a fellow casting director acknowledges that we all understand that "*actors aren't commodities—garden hoses ordered on line. A few minutes is not enough info.*"

When I was a casting executive at the ABC Television Network, I'd receive up to eighty taped auditions a week that were submitted by actors and their agents. They weren't links back then—they were the actual bulky, large video tapes. I'd watch them in the office and I'd take them home in big shopping bags to watch them on the weekends. It's a lot easier now because I just open a link, but honestly it is no less time-consuming.

The self-tape situation goes hand in hand with what one of my colleagues calls the *"twenty-four-hour audition."* What she means by that is that now that an actor can have their audition material or a script or an MP3 sent to them in a matter of seconds, they are also expected to be ready to audition in a matter of hours. Neither this fact—the insta-audition—nor the self-tape helps us as casting directors get a better idea of who you are as a human being, how you approach work, what your technique is, and so on and a lot of people feel this way. Approvals from creative teams via video who haven't met the actor in person do not allow the person viewing the tape to get any sense of how direct-able the actor is, what their rhythms are, how they work and most importantly they don't see the actor's audition process. With the in-person auditions we get to see growth; watch you transform and hear your stories. These are the things that make a director want to work with a person. How can they tell all that from a three-minute video audition? Well, they can't. But sometimes we're forced to decide just using our instincts and then we pray we're right.

While it has certainly been known to happen, very few people are hired strictly or *only* via a taped audition, so the self-tape is an important *start*. And although I've been told by an actor that they *"got hired by mystery—someone somehow saw an old safe tape and I got hired for a job I never auditioned for,"* most directors will want to meet you in person (or at the very least via an e-meeting) if the work on your self-tape is to their liking.

If a self-tape makes us "lean-in" and want more, there is almost always an in-person audition that follows. It is rarely considered more than a "pre-screen." But you should treat each self-tape like it's your final callback. And even though I've had a colleague tell me that in their experience, it's becoming more common that *"in almost every play someone gets cast via tape,"* typically the self-tape *will* be just the beginning—the part that comes before we ask you to come in to read in person.

But no matter your opinions and feelings about the self-tape method of auditioning—it is a reality now and knowing how to show your best self, physically and emotionally via self-tape is a *must*. An on-camera class can be tantamount to your success with self-tape auditions. A good one will help you with language, pace, text, memorizing, and answer every question you've ever had about how to be most effective when acting on-camera.

There are a few different schools of thought on the how-tos of the self-tape. For me personally, if I can see you and hear you and you've told me your name and height, shown me a full body shot at the start and you have a decent reader, that is enough. But I will say there is merit in taking a self-tape class. In fact, I think they should be part of every acting school's curriculum.

So, what are we looking for in the "virtual audition?" Find a room with good natural lighting and at least mostly bare walls, start your phone camera, and go to and begin. You can purchase your own backdrop and mic and maybe a light—all of which you can learn how to use via trial and error on your own or you can enlist someone to teach you. The equipment can roll right up and be stored somewhere out of sight. Or, you can go to a professional who will have lighting and backdrops and microphones and that person will shoot your audition, do your editing and create the digital link for you, too. If you like, add some graphics at the top to include your name and contact info. All of this will cost money but for a lot of actors, this is a worthy and necessary investment.

You'll want to start the tape with a "slate": "Hi, I'm Jane Smith, I'm 5'6" and I'm based in Ohio and I'm reading for the role of . . ." The camera should be pulled back to show a full body shot and then it can move in closer for the actual work and stay put.

Hold your scene pages (and music where applicable) if you must, but *make sure the pages don't block your face*. Whether you are singing or playing an instrument or speaking—doesn't matter— do *sound checks*. If the sound, or the picture for that matter, is garbled or unclear in any way, no one will watch till the end.

Don't forget, before sending the link to anyone else, send it to yourself and make sure that you can open and download it easily. In most cases if you can, others can too. Use as universal a format as possible so that no matter what device people are watching on, the link is on an easily accessible platform.

Tape while you're rehearsing the material and then watch it. That process will be informative for adjustments you might want to make. It will also provide content if you need to do any splicing and dicing, what I like to think of as "creative editing."

Judging someone on tape for a job that will be LIVE is not ideal because it's not the same medium. You might be directed to perform one way in a 2,000-seat house but that may read too big for a small screen, which is what we're watching you on, so make your acting choices accordingly. That will sometimes feel weird and wrong but go a tad smaller with how you execute your acting choices for a smaller screen.

Don't be afraid to ask questions about the audition or the material. This is especially important if you have no one representing you. Speak to or email whomever sent you your self-tape "appointment." Ask if a full script is available and what the tone and pace might be. It's very possible that after your tape is watched, you may get some notes and be asked to re-tape with those notes in mind. That's a good thing!

No matter what—if you're in the game you won't be able to avoid the self-tape, so use it to your advantage. While it may not be the preferred audition experience for the actor (and for many of the creatives, too), it is at least *one more way* to get in front of casting directors, producers and other creatives when you might not otherwise be seen. If it is the only way available to you to audition for a project, seize the opportunity. Just be sure to hone your on-camera skills so that you will be able show yourself to your best advantage when the opportunity presents itself.

16 In the Audition Room

On Being Seen

Because of my background, my heart is always with the actor first. I believe *it is your right and your job to audition wherever and whenever you can.*

After winning the Sixty-third Annual Golden Globes Award for the Best Performance by an Actor in a Motion Picture Drama for the role of Truman Capote in *Capote*, the late, great Philip Seymour Hoffman was asked what advice he might have for aspiring actors. He replied:

> When you're first starting out (and **always**, actually) you have to act wherever you can. You can't be picky. The chances to hone your craft will come in different forms. A teacher told me this once. "Even if you're auditioning for something you think you're never going to get or you read the script for an audition and you don't connect to the material—you have to go, at least while you are establishing yourself. If you get a chance to act in a room that somebody else has paid for, then you're given a free shot to practice your craft. And in that moment—act as well as you know how. Don't throw the chance away. If you leave the room or theater or wherever you are, and you've acted as well as you can, there's no way that the people who have watched you will forget it."

I mention this to point out that we know you've got to start somewhere. Thinking of the audition itself as an opportunity to work, to practice your craft, *to act*, may help alleviate your nerves and open you up in unexpected ways. Maybe even think of it as a class. We're braver when we know it's a safe environment in which to fail, but taking risks, whether it's with a partner in "Scene Study 101" or in an audition situation, will always be to your benefit.

Am I the Right "Type" for This?

The idea of type has to do with energy, skill, and personality. It also has to do with physicality. For instance, often a director has a very clear vision for the silhouette, the look of the project.

Maybe the director of *Young Frankenstein* (film or Broadway show) wants Frau Blucher to have a tall, gaunt, thin silhouette to create a sight gag when Blucher is standing next to Igor, whose silhouette might be short and round.

In a musical there is a vocal type to consider as well. An actor may have a spectacular voice but they're timbre/tone—something they have no control over—may not blend well with an actor who has already been cast—and with whom they have to sing two duets.

Everyone has different prime *type* years. You'll only be the quintessential age for Scout in *To Kill A Mockingbird,* for Kevin in the *Home Alone* franchise, for one of the high schoolers in *Dear Evan Hansen*, one of the children in *School of Rock,* or for a twenty-something role in a TV series for just so long. You'll always be aging toward a different "type" but you always are what you are—even when your age and body changes—and you can certainly have healthy careers in all the years to come. Your genetics may make you a type by virtue of your heredity but just try to be smart. Try to see yourself through eyes other than your own, then go with your gut.

If you are someone who's always felt more mature than you appear to be, then yes—it might mean a few years before you're viable for what *you* think you do best and how you come across.

This doesn't mean that someone else won't see something different in you that works for them right now.

You want to try and have some sense of how you are seen by others so you make the best use of your time as far as typing yourself in or out. Try to go gently with yourself. Err on the side of, "Well it's *possible* . . . ," rather than, "It's *usually* done *this* way and that's not *me,* so I'll skip it."

In the same way we've discussed viewing your audition as a chance to work, to practice your craft, the theory also applies to making peace with your type. Embrace it. You very well may be a certain type in the eyes of the majority, but that type has many sides and so much to say. Nurture the unique qualities you have and you may very well change peoples' minds. Two people of the same type never present in the exact same way. It's not possible. You know how no two snowflakes are exactly alike? Same with humans. Your "type" may have gotten you in the room. Now forget that and flaunt your individuality.

Be who you are. Always. Lead with that. We need to know who you are in this moment. At each stage of the audition I'm looking for something different:

STAGE 1—Did the actor prepare what was asked of them? Were they on time? Did they make smart, truthful acting choices?

STAGE 2—Did the actor learn the new material we gave them? Were they able to incorporate and MAINTAIN the adjustments and direction they were given in the room the first time? How easily can they let a rehearsed choice go and change it up with yet more and new direction?

STAGE 3—All of the above. AND how are they dealing with the nerves and the pressure and the onslaught of new people who've arrived at their final callback?

That's all you need to do in the room. Show us who you are as a human being. It is so disappointing when an actor leaves the room and I feel like I don't know anything more about them than I did when they walked in. I actually think that truly being utterly and 100 percent yourself in an audition is the hardest part. It's the hardest part in ANY public situation, isn't it? I mean, we all feel like we need permission, don't we? "Just do you!" "Just be yourself!" "JUST?" No "just" about it—it's hard to show you me! Me is none of your business! I often feel like I'm only my full true self when I'm alone, so I marvel when an actor is able to bring that in with them—and saying someone else's words while doing it! Recently a private student of mine wrote to let me know she'd booked a job and very sweetly, to thank me for the help. She said, "It helped so much to know I was allowed to imbue the role I was reading for with some of my own characteristics and opinions and traits." Yes, you're ALLOWED. You're not only allowed to, but you SHOULD also be thinking about different phrasing, and emphasis on words maybe in a way you hadn't thought of before. You're SUPPOSED to experiment with all sorts of ways to tell the story—as in "How would YOU tell the story under the circumstances of this character?" I believe that most actors make the script better when they can bring parts of themselves into it. If you're able to leave a piece of your authentic self in that room on your way out, you've succeeded. And I guarantee you've moved someone. I guarantee that whether you get this job or not, that casting director will now keep bringing you in. You are laying groundwork—good or bad—with every single audition. I guarantee the audition that got you the job was flawed. Once, I had to call an actor to come in to audition for something that started immediately. He had thirty pages of material to learn overnight. The room was packed and incredibly intimidating. I came across this actor in the hallway. He was on his knees praying. I kept walking, wanting to give him a minute before I brought him in. When I couldn't wait any longer, I touched his shoulder and asked him how he was doing. He said, "I just want to be perfect." And I'm thinking: "Kiss of death." I told him no one was interested in that. Perfect is not only dull, but it's also not possible, not HUMAN. No one wants to watch perfection. We want to see OURSELVES on that stage or screen. I saw his shoulders leave his ears. He smiled, blotted his sweaty face, drank a full bottle of water, picked up his sports coat, walked into the room, made some mistakes, but mostly KILLED IT and we told him then and there we loved him and offered him the role. And in the end? It was his imperfections that clinched it.

One more thing here. Use your common sense when deciding which auditions to attend and when choosing the role for which you are trying to get seen. Casting directors are all charged with thinking outside the box nowadays and that is not likely to change. Take chances! If there's even an outside chance you're right for a role, do your best to *get seen*.

In the Audition Room for Live Theater

If you are typed out it's because we have a responsibility to deliver what is asked for by the creative team as far as physicality and vocal range are concerned, but really that's where it ends.

Now this will be a bone of contention with some of my casting colleagues, but I say unless it's a role for a Hispanic actor who is over 6' and a tenor and you're a Caucasian soprano—be careful of typing yourself *out*. You don't know what we're looking for. Even though the breakdown information is true at the time of printing, it will often change, as things always do in a creative process. So, it follows that *what they think they want* will also change. And it does.

No one's doing a revival of a show from twenty-five years ago (or a remake of a film or TV series for that matter) the exact same way as it was originally done. This time they will want to speak to a new audience in a new era.

Use your judgment. And, especially at the beginning, *go*. Get seen.

Union and Non-Union Theater Auditions

As a casting director, I'm looking for all of you non-union newbies! If there are audition time slots that go unfilled by Equity actors at an Equity call, it's possible for them to be filled by Non-Equity Actors. I don't want to keep showing the same people to my creative teams. Show up so I know you're out there.

You may not think we really are seriously looking for actors at the required Equity calls, but I promise you, we are!

We are not allowed by the unions to begin our invited calls and appointments until we've had our required Equity calls. So, unless it says on the breakdown that the role has been cast or is on offer, all the roles are still fair game.

A huge percentage of the shows, especially the musicals on Broadway, are populated by actors first seen at open and required calls. We couldn't do the volume of work we do without those actors, so yes—we're really looking. Are there really jobs available? Is it worth your while to attend and keep attending? Yes! Yes!! Yes!!!

Required Equity Principal Auditions (EPA's) Versus Required Equity Chorus Calls

Should I go to the Equity principal audition *and* the chorus calls for the same show? Yes! Yes!! Yes!!!

I cannot speak for other casting directors. I cannot promise you that you'll attend Equity calls for productions that *don't* already have people in mind to cast or to explore. Just remember, the creative team members' visions can change in an instant and there are many roles to fill.

If you're there at the EPA it doesn't mean I won't think of you for the ensemble. And if you're there for the chorus call, it doesn't mean that I won't think you can be considered as a potential Principal. The creatives at Equity calls rarely differentiate the EPAs from the Equity chorus calls (ECCs).

Know though—that at the EPAs, *only casting is required to attend*, while at the chorus calls, someone from the creative team (music director, choreographer, and etc.) must attend.

So, at the EPA you'll get more time in the room but not the advantage of a creative team member in attendance, other than the one from the casting team.

And, at the ECC you'll get less time in the room but someone will be present who will have more casting authority than the casting person. On any given day one option may trump the other. This is why I stress the importance of *going to both when you can*.

Maybe I would have called you back but the musical director wouldn't have . . . or vice-versa. This is another example of things you won't be able to predict and that won't be consistent anyway so just make your best efforts to be seen whenever and wherever possible.

Unless you have an appointment or know you are getting one, *show up* at the required and open calls.

Making Yourself Known Industry Wide

Perhaps you want to attend an audition for the sole reason of becoming a known entity to a specific casting director, team, or office. And perhaps you don't believe that you're exactly right for a role or you think you're clearly not right for the show. I say go for it. This is another place many of my colleagues may not agree with me, but who knows? You may surprise them. You may surprise yourself!

Now a word of caution—you will want to be very careful when doing this. You will leave a lasting impression. Or, at least you'd better. And it had better be a good one! Always remember you still need to be auditioning for *that* play or television show or movie. You must intimate *that* world and even though it may be out of your comfort zone, a little outside your wheelhouse, you must do it well. For me, the bottom line is that I believe you've earned your right to be in that room. So, go. Be seen. And be great.

When the casting director is from an office that is doing many projects, for you to be seen by whomever is in that room— casting, music and dance departments, and so on,—and to leave a strong, positive impression, that can only be a good thing, right? Maybe it will turn out that you are right for that project or maybe you'll be put on file for a different one.

Point in fact; one of my first auditions out of college was an Equity chorus call for *Me and My Girl*. I believe the breakdown asked for character women, 40s—strong singers who tap. I was twenty-three and the extent of my tapping was playing a Hot Box Girl in the acclaimed Freehold Township High School production of *Guys and Dolls* (which I am not knocking—Thank you Miss Applegate, wherever you are—you made me see that stepping out of my comfort zone might just be a gateway drug). Anyway, Johnson-Liff was casting *Me and My Girl*. Guess what else they cast? *Les Misérables—and I wanted this office to know me.*

I knew no one would cast me in *Me and My Girl* but maybe, just maybe, I could somehow show some chops for both shows by singing material appropriate for *Me and My Girl*—*which is what was asked for*. Two years after that day, I went to my first open call for *Les Mis* where I found the wonderful Andy Zerman (of Johnson-Liff Casting) behind the table. Andy said, and I quote, "Merri Sugarman. Why does your name sound familiar? Oh wait. A while back you auditioned for *Me and My Girl*, right?" Groundwork. Patience. Trust that your actions today just may produce results later.

So, throw a sticky note on your picture and resume saying you'd like to also be considered for "blah-blah-blah." Put a bug in my ear. While I can't speak for other casting directors—that's perfectly fine with me.

It's worth repeating that not only is it my job to show creative new people, but it's also my goal. There is nothing I want more than for a director to look my way at a casting session and say, "Oh my God where did they come from!?! I've never seen them before. I love them!"

What's Happening on My Side of the Table

If I am in a room with people I've worked with before, I feel much freer to speak up and help educate the team regarding the actors. When a team is new to me, I tread lightly until I feel I've earned their professional respect, or until I've been asked my opinion.

Keep in mind that at the start of the audition process, certain things are asked of you, the actor. Then as the casting process evolves, I feel out what everyone's responding to—both positively and negatively—and then I may start populating the room differently throughout the process. These types of vagaries can be why actors often feel like they're getting called in for projects they don't think they are right for, and why actors cannot get seen for things they think they are perfect for.

No matter what brings you to the audition room, stay on your own path—show *yourself* off. Don't worry so much about what you think we want. Worry about how to show us who you are. Your internal thought—instead of "I wonder what they are looking for" should be "I can't wait to go in and show them who I am." Who you *are* and how *you* interpret the work is what we find interesting!

Part 5
After the Audition

17 Booking It—Or Not

The following is one of my very favorite self-submission success stories. This actor didn't *exactly* follow the playbook I outlined for you in the previous pages (but you please do!), but it illustrates that your dream job can come to you seemingly out of the blue and more quickly than in any of your wildest dreams.

A few years ago, I was sitting at my desk trying to catch up on my mail. I opened the manila envelope that was on the top of the stack and out of it dropped a DVD labeled "*John Doe—Any State College* Senior Choir Showcase" (Not the actor's real name or the or the school's real name). I popped the disc into the computer and on the screen, a very fuzzy picture appeared of what I *thought* were four guys singing *Sherry* from *Jersey Boys* and doing the exact choreography from the Broadway show. Included in the envelope was a handwritten letter from "John Doe" asking me to watch the video and to please consider him for *Jersey Boys*. So, I watched. I mean—I tried to watch. It was out of focus and shot from far away. And by the way, the note did not mention which one of the four guys was him! The sound was bad, but I could tell that whoever was singing Frankie Valli's part was doing so beautifully. So, I called "John Doe," got his voice mail and left a message saying—Hi, it's Merri Sugarman at Tara Rubin Casting. I'm watching your DVD and I wanted to mention a few things. (A) Which one are you? I am hoping you're the one on the far right and please tell me the truth 'cause I'll know if you're not. (B) You are doing a public performance of Sergio Trujillo's Tony-nominated choreography. I think that might be against the law unless you have permission. But I'm not sure. (C) Can you come in and audition for the role of Joe Pesci and to cover Frankie for the national tour of *Jersey Boys*? Thanks—I will send an appointment time via email.

So, I met that very nervous kid with that gorgeous voice and I moved him forward to meet the creative team. He did a lot more singing and reading and dancing—including the hip-hop combination that continues to fluster and confound the best of dancers—and he was the epitome of grace throughout the whole audition process.

I had to tell him later that we weren't moving him forward at that point, that he'd done beautifully, and that we'd keep him on our radar for future replacements. Two weeks after that, the needs of the show suddenly changed, and we had him back in—this time with the director and producers in the room and following that audition, I was told to make him an offer—for the *Broadway* company.

Now usually the guys who book roles like that audition many times, over the course *of years*. For *Jersey Boys*, they are very often graduates of what we call *Frankie Camp*—a three-day, paid, by invitation-only, intensive workshop where actors work with the associate team—the directors, music directors, dance department and the *Jersey Boys* vocal coach. It's a big investment the producers make so we can help actors develop and get ready to possibly play that very demanding part. The graduates then show their work to the production supervisor, the music director, and the choreographer and we put them on video for the director and for everyone else who may need to approve them later—often including Frankie Valli. Then we wait until there is an appropriate opening and then they audition. Again.

So, there's this kid, "John Doe," who had no union card, who'd only graduated from college a few months ago, and had been told he's not going to go any further in the audition process. And then I got to call him to start the actual offer process. The first step in the offer process is to check availability—he said he'd just signed on to go out on a non-Equity tour of *I Love A Piano* and I asked if he'd rather join the Broadway company of *Jersey*

Boys instead. I offered him the role of Joe Pesci, and understudy to Frankie Valli. There was dead silence on the other end. I asked if he was still there and heard a small whimper which grew into an excited scream of "yesssssssss!" He then started tripping over his words and talking a mile a minute about his contract with *I Love A Piano*. He was utterly panicked. I told him we'd figure it all out together. Once again, he started whimpering and I again asked if he was okay. Between the tears and the sniffling, he managed to choke out, "I'm just so happy! And it's my birthday!" Moments like that are my very favorite part of the job.

Why Didn't I Get the Job?

Auditions are a very human, flawed business. You have no control over the way you're being perceived. While that is a challenging notion, the very fact that it's not a science should free you up to show us who you are and what you can do with the material. The audition process is a creative work in progress in much the same way as the casting process.

When I start a job, I sit down with the creative team and talk about concepts and prototypes. They tell us what they want the project to look like design-wise and, if it's a musical, how it should sound. Maybe they want it to feel like a silent film from the 1930s or maybe it will be set in the sewers of Paris or maybe the movie will be set in the woods of Wisconsin during a blizzard. So, they want to see people who could be, or at least *feel like* they might be inherently of that world.

Of course, as an actor, you believe you can be of *any* world. Well yes, you can, if the people behind the table see it that way. The comments from the creatives can go something like, "I love her but she feels too twenty-first century millennial," or "She sounds so educated—is anyone going to believe she never made it past third grade?"—and so on.

With television, if you have a great audition, and don't book the show, it's possibly because you are not a good fit with the rest of the cast being assembled. While your read was fantastic, someone on the creative team might feel nobody is going to buy that you are the sister of the actress just cast in the starring role.

Everyone on the creative team will undoubtedly have completely different opinions and needs. It's my job to present candidates who come closest to fulfilling the ideal—as a whole—as envisioned by all the members of the creative team.

Honestly, half the time we think we've cast the show and we're done. We congratulate each other. We're excited. Then, after having spent three hours walking and talking around a table or looking at a board with all the contenders' pictures displayed under the different roles to be cast, and everyone is putting on their coats to leave, the casting director may suddenly realize someone we all just decided to make an offer to, isn't the best option, that someone else will be more useful in more case scenarios, for any number of reasons. Let's say we forgot to discuss the fact that someone we've already cast would be out for a month because they have a prior commitment and we've decided we want them badly enough to make that work. So now the actor we were going to hire to cover that actor is in use as the cover during that month and now we have to cast someone who can cover *that* actor. And so, we see suddenly that someone who was about to get an offer is no longer useful to us—our needs have changed. And, someone who was never even discussed for the final cut, is now again being considered. Or, the next day someone had second thoughts about the final choices and we're back to square one and, again, someone who, in theory, had a job is now off the table because someone else ticked more boxes. It's brutal, isn't it?

There are so many frustrating scenarios:

Maybe I'm casting a Pilot but the actor we all like has a "quote" (salary on the last job) that is too high for the budget, so we focus on a different actor who is more affordable. That actor might be you.

Maybe, while you've been auditioning, a project has suddenly become cast-contingent, meaning the theater owner is having second thoughts and will only welcome this project to the building with a star in the lead role—one who they believe will guarantee ticket sales. Also known as "good box office." So, while you've been working very hard learning your sides and your music and coming in for auditions, the producers have asked me to seek out actors who will help keep the lights on, the seats full and the box-office revenue strong. Now it's back to the drawing board for me and you're out of the running. We may, however, come back to you in the Fall when that star leaves or for the touring company or keep auditioning you but now it's to understudy the lead instead of to play the role.

Maybe you come in to audition on a Wednesday and I think you've nailed it. Then on Thursday you come in again for the creative team. We are in the exact same room, you're wearing the exact same clothes, and you're performing the exact same material. Again, I think you're brilliant. Then my director turns to me and says "I know you love her, but I'm not a fan." Art isn't easy.

Sometimes, when you hear that catch-all phrase—that you just weren't a good fit—the harsh reality is that in a tiny percentage of circumstances, it meant that you quite literally weren't a good fit. For Broadway show replacements, sometimes there may not be time to build costumes from the ground up for a new actor, so word will come down from the wardrobe department that (all other skill sets being equal, of course) the replacement can't be taller than 5'7" and no smaller or larger than a certain clothing size.

Or, maybe with a long-running show—when you can't understand why you're not being seen when you're *exactly* like the person who's currently playing the role—it's because I was told to go a different way. But how would you know that? Sadly, you won't.

An actor once asked me why he'd been clearly in the mix—for *years*—for a certain role in the Broadway company of a show I was casting but could not get seen for the touring company when the same role came open. Good question. Different companies of the same shows may be cast differently. There is no "formula" and they are not "cookie-cutter."

For one thing, in the long run, replacements need to be a good fit for the *current company*. You may have been right a year ago when you weren't available to come in but now, when that track is again open for a replacement—you are not right for *that* moment, for *that current* cast.

In addition to all that, sometimes we have different criteria for different companies of the same show. For example— the Broadway company is cast, and the mix is successful, so consequently we try to maintain that cast type-wise as we replace. If it ain't broke, don't fix it. But then we go on to cast the Las Vegas company which is in a *huge* house, and we cast *for the Las Vegas audience* who want to get in, see the show and get back out to the tables. So, the cast there may be a little slicker and tend to skew a bit younger than the Broadway cast. They may even do a slightly different—maybe a slightly cut-down version of the show itself. All of those variables bring different casting needs with them.

And just as Las Vegas is different than Broadway, national tours have their own particular needs. While we always pay attention to actors' temperaments, nowhere is that truer than for the road companies. We strive for what we hope will be a cohesive unit, a real family, for tours in particular.

On tour some cast members may need to get up at four in the morning, twice a week, every week, to be ready to sing at six in the morning on the local network segment shown during *Good Morning America*. Those actors need to be scintillating and articulate when being interviewed by the local arts news anchor. In short—they need to be the living, breathing ambassadors of the show. Maybe the director feels that Actor A is great onstage, but isn't charming or talkative enough to be the public face of the touring company—the *person* trying to get people to buy tickets.

And on tour, even with internet chat and cheap flights, some actors feel isolated when they are far from home. They can feel out of the loop of consideration for other auditions and new projects so they become unhappy and don't thrive in that environment. Tours also require actors who will be able to read reviews and be okay with them—because sometimes there is an opening night *every* week! It takes a certain kind of temperament to handle life on the road well. And so it goes. You won't always know the how, what, where and when of why you didn't book the job and you'll have to figure out how to let it all go and live with that reality.

There's no easy answer as to why you did or did not get the job. Chances are, in both cases, you'll never know why. More often than not, it's a crazy confluence of circumstances that leads to your booking the job. Or not. You cannot imagine how many stars have to align for you to get an offer. Considerations being discussed are that which you'll never know about and wouldn't be anywhere on your radar. Nor should they be. It's good you don't have to imagine—because I'm about to name just a few. Assuming everyone who's seen your work and/or been involved with your audition process so far are in agreement you're capable of playing the role, they agree you have the—acting chops, right attitude, interesting and appropriate look, now the discussion begins about your age and your height as it pertains to the actors with whom you'll be working. Do we believe they're both college sophomores and do they have chemistry? Is she THAT much better than the lead producer's daughter—whom it'd benefit us ALL to cast instead? We know the lead in this play is getting married two months into the run; is the person we want to cast to cover them a quick enough study so they'll own the role by the time they have to go on in the lead actor role or do we play it safe and cast the actor who played the role in another production, and whom we all like, and who needs the insurance weeks? Let's say there's a height and weight limit. The reason for maximum heights and weights is usually because another actor has to lift them, or carry them—sometimes while singing an aria or trudging up a mountain. Well, we just cast the role of the "carrier" with someone much physically smaller than we'd anticipated so now the actor we like, who has to adhere to a height and weight limit—and someone who was well within the limits before we cast this other role, is no longer in the running. Maybe the role gets cut entirely but there are legalities that don't allow us to say so just yet. Once I heard a director say, "He's GREAT—best person we saw! Problem is that on a tour, I need him to help sell tickets. That means appearing on local morning shows and the guy just isn't all that charming when he's not on stage. Maybe that more out-going actor we saw a few weeks ago serves us better." I mean … RIGHT? It's so WRONG that the most talented, most worthy person is not getting this part! PLUS—you've almost definitely been videoed (with your permission of course) throughout your audition process so that anyone who has casting approval and wasn't able to be present for your audition(s) can see your final audition. And they're basing THEIR decisions on that video ALONE, while everyone else has had the benefit of directing you, observing your style and prep work, seeing how you take adjustments—in the room, multiple times over the course of weeks or even months. ALL of that informed everyone's approval! And now here's this person who just didn't like what they saw on that one tape . . . You will rarely know the WHY of any of it and that is NOT easy—but it is what it is.

Let's focus on why you aren't getting the job. What is it about the audition room that scares you? I would tell them to get back in class, stop focusing so hard on getting the job and focus on finding your joy in the room. The most interesting thing about telling a client they didn't receive a job is that every job and client reacts differently. Every job has a different significance to the client and each receives good and bad news differently. I certainly prefer telling them they got the job but when I have to tell them they didn't, I always try to focus on the fact that the job just wasn't meant to be and because they didn't get it, new doors will open.
JENNIFER NAMOFF, *Talent Manager*

Navigating an Offer

When an offer does come your way, here are some basic questions you will want to ask:

- What is the salary?
- What is the per diem (if applicable)?
- What are the health benefits and or pension contributions?
- What is the length of the contract?
- Can I break this contract for any reason? Will I get contractual "outs?" (Approved reasons to be able to break a contract.)
- If I don't have automatic "outs" on this type of contract, is that negotiable?
- Is this a role that warrants a discussion about billing?

An actor without representation will want to have someone with some experience, for instance, an attorney to look over the contract. If you have no representation, try to speak to your union representative or someone who has worked under this type of contract before who can point out some of the pitfalls that they may have encountered. There are many different types of contracts and you only start to know the right questions to ask and what your needs may be during a job when you start working and talking with other actors and industry professionals.

Sometimes, an actor gets signed by an agent simply by asking them to negotiate a contract for them. You may give up some percentage of your salary as payment for their negotiating skills, but the bonus is, now you've got an agent.

The main thing to remember is that every time you audition, and book the job—or not—if you take the time to analyze everything that transpired during the audition process, you will learn something. And every lesson learned along the way will make you better prepared for all the auditions to follow.

18 The First Day of School

Let's talk about day one of your new job. You've worked really hard to get to this place and it's scary and exciting. But the work actually starts before you show up for the first day with your new colleagues—there's work to be done once you have been hired but haven't yet started rehearsal.

From the second you've received your script, get down to work. Highlight your lines. Write your cues on index cards followed by your lines in as large a print as you need. Record your scenes with someone saying the lines and leaving space for you to respond with your lines. There's even an APP for that—whatever works for you. Just be as familiar as possible with your lines and music.

It behooves you to find a disciplined way of working when you are not on set, or in a play and have some downtime. For example, if you book a television show, it's very possible that you could have a completely different script waiting for you when you arrive and/or new pages with changes every day. Particularly with episodic television, everything is very fast and change is a constant. Being as familiar as possible with your lines allows you the freedom to really be present and able to listen and take in blocking (where to move and when), acting adjustments and direction during rehearsal. You'll want to be able to do all this in as economical and efficient way as possible without having to ask a ton of questions. Don't be afraid to try stuff. Go with your gut. If you do something wrong, or take the character in a direction that isn't wanted, trust me, you'll hear about it.

Television

Whether you've booked a job on a television show as a series regular (you're part of the principal cast that comes back week after week), as a recurring role (a character that is part of the ongoing series, but is in just two or three or a few more episodes per season) or as a guest character specific to one episode only, you will still be under the same type of casting scrutiny at the start of the show. It may be the first day of school for you, but you still need to demonstrate that you belong in that room.

The Table Read

The table read happens on the first day when the entire cast and crew gather around a table (hence the name) to read through an episode for the first time. Executives from the studio and the network will be there. The writers and producers will be there. And sometimes the casting directors will be, too.

The network and studio people are concerned with everything—content, length, appropriate language and most importantly for you, they're taking a long hard look at casting. This is the first time they will be able to evaluate the assembled cast as a whole. Did they choose right? Is the chemistry promising? Is the director happy with the actors? Does anyone need to be replaced?

When it's an established series and the executives are looking specifically at the guest actors at the table reads, if the actor isn't "delivering" at the table read, most creatives will understand that it often takes a rehearsal process to get to the finished product and usually all is well in the end. But also, if it's clear a casting mistake has been made, if an actor doesn't "bring the funny" or if the actor just isn't portraying a character as hoped, then the casting director might need to be ready to show the team a few new actors that very day.

The Shoot

Now the table read is over and you're still on board, rehearsal begins. In addition, you'll have scheduled costume fittings and hair and makeup sessions.

The order of how things will go now starts to vary. You might rehearse the scene and shoot it then and there. You may need to go to a different location and film an "exterior" shot (one that is out of doors or not on set). The shooting will rarely take place in the scripted order. That can be challenging for the actor. Sometimes you'll have to play the character as they are at the end of the show at the very beginning of the shoot. And the schedule will often change at a moment's notice so you'll want to be as prepared as possible for that eventuality.

When you're cast in one of the television shows that films in front of a live studio audience, the culmination of all the rehearsals you've had will be performing the TV show as if it's a play for an audience that is right in front of you. Expect there to be breaks in the action and that scenes may be repeated as necessary.

Film

Your preparation process should be basically the same process as outlined in the television section. For a film, sometimes there won't be a table read. In fact, the full cast and crew rarely will be in the same room at the same time. You'll just start with a rehearsal for the scenes on the schedule that day and then do the shoot itself. While there is some rehearsal time, usually the camera will start rolling and you'll begin the scene and continue to do as many takes as the director sees fit. And just the same as with television, scenes typically shoot out of order.

Theater

Plays

The first day and every day, you start by signing in on the call sheet (by the way this is the same for film and television; this is what let's everyone know you're on the premises) on the call board. Be sure to read every piece of information on the call board that day and every day going forward. You will find it an invaluable resource and you will be expected to know any and all of the information posted there for your benefit.

If this is an Equity show, the stage manager will gather the cast and an "Equity Deputy" will be elected by the cast. This is the person the actors go to throughout the run if they have any questions or concerns about labor rules, hours, harassment, etc. Etiquette says one should really go to the production stage manager first to see if the issue can be resolved without union intervention but the Equity Deputy will be your liaison to your union representatives.

Play rehearsals sometimes start with a full read-through of the script with the full company. Sometimes you're broken out into smaller groups to start. This usually takes place in a studio where the floor will be diagramed with colored tape approximating the stage dimensions and locations of the different set pieces and areas, for instance, the bedroom, the kitchen, and so on. I recommend being off book (having your part memorized) as much as possible so you are free to absorb your blocking (stage directions) and direction.

You'll know when and if you're called for rehearsal based on the information you get from stage management. Make sure you read all communications promptly and thoroughly as things change frequently.

Musicals

As always in any legit theater situation, you start the day by signing in at the call board. If you're not signed in, technically speaking, you're not there.

For musical theater, it's rare for there to be a table read. Instead, the first day of rehearsal usually takes the form of a "meet and greet" which is conducted at the start of the day. It has the feel of a social mixer since there is typically food and soft drinks and everyone takes a turn introducing themselves to the crowd. The gathering will include practically everyone involved in the project—the producers and creative team, the actors, crew and musicians, the public relations team, the advertising and social media team, marketing, merchandising, and so on.

After the Meet and Greet you will most likely separate into different rehearsal studios where the floors will be marked and taped off just as they are for plays. Some folks will go to work on choreography, some will do scene work and others will begin to learn the score. I highly recommend recording the music sessions. Make sure to get your harmony parts recorded, learn the measure numbers that indicate where you come in and where you start, and so on. Mark your music and scripts as you are given directions. Use a pencil with an eraser.

At the end of each day, you'll be expected to go home and continue to work so that you have the material memorized as much as possible for the next rehearsal. And if not by then, certainly very soon thereafter. If you don't know your stuff when run-throughs of each act begin, it can hold up the work.

Eventually, for both plays and musicals, you'll move into the theater and start technical rehearsals. In tech, sound, lighting, set pieces, props, automation and all the other production properties are added to the equation. You'll do a lot of standing around under hot lights waiting for the design team to do their thing—focus lights, discuss colors, sort out cues of all types, evaluate the wardrobe, makeup and hair, and figure out how to do quick changes and set changes and so on. This is also when you'll start getting familiar with the traffic patterns and timing of your movements both on and off stage. It's nerve wracking and fun and exhausting and it's *really* a time when you'll want to take extra care with yourselves health-wise!

19 Alternate Career Path?

While I certainly came into my own professionally in Los Angeles and had a mostly very happy existence there for eight years (up until then, it was the longest I'd ever stayed anywhere in my adult life), I never felt like my skin fit quite right there. I think I started, albeit subconsciously, yearning for New York pretty quickly into my time there. Things change. What feels right and good in one moment suddenly feels wrong and bad in the next. I was older and wiser and maybe not as brave as I'd been when I'd first moved out to Los Angeles, but I knew I needed to see what was next for me. I had all the usual self-doubt. "What was I thinking leaving such a great job?" "Was I really going to try and reinvent myself all over again?" And I floundered for a while longer and then after a lot of reaching out to family and friends for moral support, I decided to move back to New York. I quit my job at ABC Television amid much protestation from people who thought they knew better about what was good for me than I did. So many well-intentioned folks told me that I was at the top of my game and that if I left, I'd never work in casting again. I knew they might be right, but I also knew I had to go. I had to take that risk and make some changes.

When you're in crisis, it's very interesting and more significantly, really hard to watch and see who sticks by you and who falls by the wayside. You realize fairly quickly that as an adult you're pretty much on your own. But it can be very freeing too. And trust me—you come out the other side wiser and stronger and with coping skills you didn't know you had, still scared but somehow energized too because you survived. I left Los Angeles with a little money and a serious case of "burn-out."

Just as I was settling in back home in New York, I got a call from a former employer in Los Angeles offering me a job as an on-set coach to an actor for a television movie that was shooting in Vancouver. It was a three to four-month shoot, the pay was excellent, and the work was intriguing. I was flattered to be asked and knew enough to jump at the opportunity. So, with my new apartment still littered with unpacked boxes, I renewed my passport and embarked on a new adventure.

By the way, the naysayers were wrong when they said I'd made a mistake leaving Los Angeles. It was those very people who hired me for the coaching job in Vancouver. I was still a valuable asset to them—just in a different way. Sometimes, yes, it'll be a disaster and you may burn some bridges, but mostly, when you follow your instincts, when you trust yourself, it will lead you in the right direction. I learned so much about coaching and teaching from that film and will always be grateful that it came into my life at that critical juncture.

When the movie wrapped, I went home to New York and shortly thereafter got involved with a nonprofit organization that helped bring after-school arts programs to places that couldn't otherwise afford them. I met a kid who was interested in casting, so I called Tara Rubin of Tara Rubin Casting—the person who'd cast me in practically everything I'd ever done as an actor—and asked if she needed an intern. She didn't. What she did need was a casting director and she made me an offer. I gratefully accepted and haven't looked back since.

If you're anything like me, you have well-intentioned friends and family insisting that you should have something to fall back on. And you have industry pros and teachers tell you the exact opposite—that you must be focused on one thing, twenty-four hours a day, seven days a week, blinders on, shutting out everything but the pursuit of an acting job. In a way, they're both right, but the trick is to find the balance that works for you.

Dancers, just like all other professional athletes, enter into careers knowing they need to think about alternate ways to make a living as they age. The body betrays and simply won't allow you to continue to do the same things you've been able to do in the past, so dancers learn early to think about what will come later as a second career. It really is no different for actors.

What else are *you* interested in? Performing may be your current love, but it may not be your last love. So, what else gets your creative juices flowing? Stage management? Casting, maybe? Teaching? By the way, the old adage "Those who can't, teach" is bullshit. Those who *can*, teach. Great teachers are the bedrock of *everything*.

If you're still "spinning your wheels" after a certain amount of time with no success—and the amount of time that will be "enough" will be different for everyone—and I am speaking of success in whatever way that means to *you*—then it is time to sit down and ask yourself the hard questions.

How, exactly, do you measure success? What specific things do you want to accomplish within the next two years? Ten years? In your career in the arts? *Are you happy?*

When I realized I was unhappy with my life in Los Angeles, I began asking myself what would make me happy. That was hard because if I really answered honestly, it might mean I would have to change the course of my whole life—which might mean I'd be embarrassed—I'd have to admit I'd failed in some way. Or that everything that led me to this point was a waste of time.

I promise you though, it's not about failure. It's about maturation. It's about growth. It's about feeling safe and satisfied and in control of your own destiny. It's really scary. And really worth it. Failing isn't *not* meeting your goals, but not *knowing* when to change course and move on.

To be pursuing *anything* that takes hard work is worth it—and anything *worth* pursuing *does* take hard work. But *not* being passionate about your career is the biggest dead end ever and that really is a waste of valuable time.

It may very well be that at some time, or from time to time, you choose to put your acting career on hold. Life happens. Your kids need to eat. You take a job so you can feed them. But at some point, they'll be able to feed themselves and the next chapter will be *yours*. By then you're older and wiser and who knows? Maybe you will have grown into your type and you're even more marketable than you were two, five or ten years ago. And if you're reading this because you've reached the time to restart your acting career, good for you. It is never too late to switch it up or start fresh. Welcome back.

At the end of the day, if you really think about it in a practical way, you'll realize that picking up different skill sets along the way can't hurt. Most actors have a plethora of talents—public speaking, exceptional interpersonal communication skills, an empathetic nature, and *heart*. While you're on this journey, pay attention to and develop a curiosity about other jobs in the field. Should you decide to transition to another area, those careers in the industry can provide an equally (or maybe even more) rewarding life.

20 That's a Wrap

I'm going to wrap this up with an audition success story that I hope you'll take to heart. Although I can't take any credit for how this actor conducted himself during the audition process, it makes me proud every time I think about it. Proud of him, proud of his success and proud of my career choice. I think you'll recognize that many of the fundamental principles I've been recommending throughout this book are the backstory here. It reaffirms and demonstrates my belief that talent is a gift you're given, but persistence and hard work is the gift you give yourself—because that is what will help you develop your talents and survive and thrive in your chosen career as an actor.

I had the privilege of being the casting director for *Ain't Too Proud—The Life and Times of the Temptations,* with music and lyrics by The Temptations and a book by Dominique Morisseau. The show is based on the story of the singing group The Temptations and was directed by Des McAnuff and choreographed by Sergio Trujillo and opened on Broadway at the Imperial Theater in 2019. All of the actual The Temptations are singularly talented individuals and finding actors who could convincingly portray them proved to be a truly daunting task. In the end, we were blessed with an embarrassment of riches talent-wise and the show opened to great success.

Now that's a great problem to have—but a successful show brings with it the ongoing challenge of finding replacement casts for the Broadway production and future touring productions. One of the biggest challenges for any show is to find actors who can take on the role of a principal character Stand-By. But now we're talking *The Temptations*. These actors need to not only play two or three of the classic Temptations but they must also *own* the roles of those exceptionally talented men who all have very different skill sets and distinct personalities. *True* triple threats were needed and if a suggestion for a potential candidate came my way, I explored it. Not too far into the run, a recommendation for an actor came to me by way of a producer pal. The actor had been working for a while but I didn't know him. I investigated and what I learned seemed promising, so I called him in for an audition. I gave him a ton of material to learn—six cuts of six different songs and nine scenes for three separate roles. When he came in for his pre-screen audition, I honestly thought I wasn't seeing or hearing right. He was just that good.

I brought him back for the musical supervisor and the musical director and the associate director. They saw the potential, too. We sent the actor through to the dance call. He was given average scores by the associate choreographer. Keep in mind this was Sergio Trujillo's Tony Award-winning choreography and included knee turns and splits. As a group we all decided he should be seen by the full team. He came in and he was fine, but not nearly as electric as he'd been at his first audition. It was decided that he was worth keeping in the mix for some time down the line—maybe for the tour or a Broadway replacement, but that he wasn't "there" just yet.

That same day, one of the Broadway actors in *Ain't Too Proud* gave their notice and we suddenly found ourselves in need of a stand-by in rehearsal for the Broadway company *asap*. This news came on a Friday. After lengthy discussions over the weekend, it was decided we'd re-visit the aforementioned actor and bring him back in on Tuesday. *And* we added *another* character for him to prepare, so he was given even more material to learn.

So, only three days after his first audition for the creative team, the associate team spent three hours with him before his final callback working scenes and songs. The music department took the time to play him some real Temptations tracks and Sergio himself came in and worked with him. Sergio closed the curtains on the wall of mirrors and (with the Broadway Dance Captain sitting by Sergio's side rather than up in front doing the choreography along with the actor as is the usual practice) watched as this young man went through two very complicated combinations, sweated through his shirt and fully split his pants seam open. Sergio asked, "Now why didn't you dance that way for me last week?" And the actor replied, "I don't know. I think I was too much inside my own head."

During this whole process I kept thinking how much we were putting him through—the emotional torture that is the audition process. We gave him a break to gather his wits about him before the rest of the creative team arrived. All fifteen of them. All there to see one actor. So . . . no pressure.

I stepped out to go to the restroom and I saw the actor sitting on a bench in the hallway with his sport coat barely covering the split in his pants seam. I asked if he was ok and if he needed anything. He said he was "just a perfectionist" and was really worried about "messing up." And my answer to that was the same then as it would be now—no one is interested in perfection. It's dull. I gave him a hug and told him to try and have some fun and said, "You wanna star in a Broadway musical? Go in there and be a star. You know, like you are when you're alone and just fantasizing about it." And he hit it out of the park. I mean the guy was grace personified. He listened. He made adjustments. He stayed present. And when he left, Des, the director said, "slam dunk." Casting director Tara Rubin said, "*This actor came to book.*" And he did.

I bumped into him not long after that and I asked him if he'd learned the entire packet of material we had sent to him. It was close to *ninety* pages even though in the first two auditions we hadn't even asked him for half of it nor did we on the day of his final callback. And he answered, "Yes. Because I told myself if I got the job, I'd be halfway there already when I started." By the way, that actor was later cast in the first national tour of *Ain't Too Proud* in the role he was a stand-by for on Broadway.

I promise that his attitude and work ethic is the reason that that actor will continue to book work for the rest of his life. On that eight-hour day he demonstrated the grit, fortitude, determination and preparation that it takes to make it in this business. Those present that day won't soon forget it.

I can only hope that that story and the tenets set forth in this book will solidify for you the idea that work begets work, that the cream rises to the top, that kindness counts and that failure or success is all in your perspective.

Index

A . . . My Name is Alice   60
ABC Television Network   6, 65,
        118, 151
Actors Equity Association—
        The Union for Stage
        Actors   62–3
after-school programs   37
agents   5, 8, 16–17, 22, 28, 32–5,
        41–2, 51–9, 66, 81, 84,
        87, 90–1, 94, 99, 111–13,
        115, 118, 144
*Ain't Too Proud—The Life and Times
        of the Temptations*   155
Aladdin   54
alternate career path   151–4
Aspects of Love   5, 19
audition notices   83
auditions
    clothes   109–10
    internet   113–15
        insta-stars   114
        social media   113
    overcoming nerves   106–7
    performance, adjusting for
        audition room   108
    specialty songs   104
    transposing the song   105
    video auditions   110–11

Backstage.com   59
The Book of Mormon   54
breakdowns   83, 86–7

Broadway league local
        venues   29–30
    large-scale touring
        productions   29
Broadway touring shows   30
Brooks, Mel   99
Bullets Over Broadway   54
Burt Reynolds Institute for Theater
        Training (BRITT)   60

cabarets   21, 28, 113
Caird, John   13–14
callbacks   88–9, 92–4
casting director's role   83
casting executives   85, 91
casting process   1, 25–6, 84–6, 88,
        94–5, 130, 137
Cats   12
Chicago   15
    Lyric Opera   112
    regional and repertory
        theaters   18
child actor career
    agent or manager   41–2
    legit (licensed and franchised)
        clients   42
    resume   41–2
Cirque du Soleil   18
comedy clubs   28
commercials   27–8, 32–3, 50–1
community and dinner theater,
        auditions for   1, 25–7, 29

Contact 54
continuing education
    books 71–2
    films 73–4
    plays 72–3
    recommended reading and
        viewing 71–4
    television 74–5
Crazy For You 54
curious kids 35–43

Dreamworks Studios 6, 65, 91
Drowsy Chaperone 54

Edinburgh Fringe Festival 31
Equity 11, 26, 59, 60, 86–7
    auditions 56
Equity Chorus Calls (ECCs) 127–8
Equity Deputy 148
Equity Membership Candidate
    (EMC) 62
Equity Principal Auditions
    (EPA) 127–8
extra work, film and television 50

5th Avenue Theater in Seattle 18
film 94–5
    feature and independent
        films 34
Fosse, Bob 60
Fowler, Beth 60

generals 111
Good Morning America 141
The Groundlings 29
guest and co-star roles 92
Guthrie in Minneapolis 18

hierarchy of network casting
        executives 92
Hoffman, Philip Seymour 122

Imperial Theater 155
improv 28–9

adult continuing education
    classes 28

Jersey Boys 135
jingles 32–3
Johnson-Liff Casting 12

keeping in touch with contacts 22–3

large-scale touring
    productions 29
Las Vegas 18, 140
Leeds, Andrew Harrison 35–7
legit theater, audition process 87–8
Les Misérables 5, 11–13, 35, 42, 129
Lincoln Center Library 71
local acting opportunities 24
local dance studios 25, 29
local theater auditions 25
looping 33
Los Angeles 5, 15
    improv schools 17

McAnuff, Des 155
McCoo, Marilyn 60
managers 42, 51, 53–9, 84, 87,
    90–1, 111–12, 143, 148
Me and My Girl musical 36, 129
Mean Girls 54
Minneapolis 15, 29
Miss Saigon 12, 39, 40, 42
Morisseau, Dominique 155
The Music Man 54

National Alliance for Musical
    Theatre (NAMT) 31
negotiations 92–3
networking 24, 65–9
network test 92
New England Theater Conference
    (NETCs) 30
New York 4–5, 7, 11, 14–18, 24,
    29, 31, 36, 71, 79, 112–13,
    151–2

open calls and actor's Equity
union calls   16
working as an extra   16
New York Musical Festival
(NYMF)   31
Nicholas Nickleby   13
Nicholaw, Casey   54
Nickelodeon   91
non-Equity theater   61–3, 127,
136

Off-Off Broadway, Off-Broadway,
and Broadway   32
Oklahoma!   54
open call   88
auditions   87
for local shows   25
Oregon   15
Shakespeare Festival   18
Outer Critics Circle Award   13

Pesci, Joe   135
Phantom of the Opera   12
Philadelphia   15
Playbill.com   59, 87
pre-screen auditions   91–2, 94
The Producers   54
professional regional theaters   29
The Prom   54

reels   51
Reigel, Eden   35
Reigel, Lenore   35
Reigel, Sam   35
Renaissance festivals   31
representation and submissions
actor's representation   53
agency   57
agents   54–5
classes and workshops   58
managers   55
meetings with potential
representation   58–9
submissions   55–8

required equity chorus calls   127–
8
resumes   48–51
Reynolds, Burt   60
Reynolds Institute for Theater
Training (BRITT)   60
Royal Shakespeare Company   13
Rubin, Tara   7, 79, 152, 157

Saturday Night Live   42
The Scottsboro Boys   54
Screen Actors Guild-American
Federation of Television
and Radio Artists
(SAG-AFTRA) for film,
television and voice
actors   63–4
screen test process   94
Seattle   15
Second City   29
self-tape audition
on-camera class   119
Shakespeare festivals   31
Show Boat   54
Simon, Neil   100
Something Rotten   54
Southeastern Theater Conference
(SETCs)   30
Spamalot   54
special skills on resume   50–1
Starlight Express   12
Steel Pier   54
Stratford Festival   18, 31
STRAWHATS   30
Stroman, Susan   54
student films   33–4
summer camps   4, 11, 13, 37
Summer Theater (Summer
Stock)   30
Sunset Boulevard   12

table read   146–7
Taft Hartley   64
Tara Rubin Casting   152

Teddy & Alice musical   36
television   17, 27–8, 32, 63–4,
        84–5, 91–4, 109,
        146–7
television and film   84–5
The Temptations   155
The Tonight Show   42
Tony Voter tickets   8
Touchstone   91
Trujillo, Sergio   135, 155–7

union and non-union theater
        auditions   127
unions   60–4
    Actors Equity Association-
        The Union for Stage
        Actors   62–3

Equity Membership
        Candidate (EMC)   62
    joining Equity   62–3
Upright Citizens Brigade   29

voice lessons and acting
        classes   5
voice-overs   32–3

Warner Brothers   91
Webber, Andrew Lloyd   5
workshops   2, 7, 37, 41, 58, 113,
        136

Young Frankenstein   99, 123

Zerman, Andy   13